LOST LESSONS 3

A DEVOTIONAL BY TEENS FOR TEENS

By
Dr. Randy T. Johnson
and
David Rutledge

© 2011 Randy Johnson

Copyright 2011 Randy Johnson

Published by:
Rochester Media LLC
P.O. Box 80002
Rochester, MI 48308
248-429-READ
www.rochestermedia.com

All rights reserved. No part of this book may be reproduced or transmitted in any form or by any means including, but not limited to, electronic or mechanical, photocopying, recording, or by any information storage or retrieval system without written permission from the publisher, except for the inclusion of brief quotations in review.

All scripture quotations, unless otherwise indicated, are taken from Holy Bible, New International Version NIV R (Reserved Symbol?) copyright C (Copyright Symbol?) 1973, 1978, 1984 by International Bible Society.

Author: Dr. Randy Johnson, David Rutledge
Cover Design & Formatting: Jamieson Design
Caricatures: Don Pinsent

First U.S. Edition Year 1st Edition was Published

Summary: Christian devotional based on the television series Lost ®

ISBN: 978-1466461826

1. Christian Living, Spiritual Growth, Christianity, Religion

For current information about releases by Dr. Randy Johnson or other releases from Rochester Media, visit our website: http://www.rochestermedia.com

Printed in the United States of America

Preface

LOST Lessons was written by Randy Johnson and David Rutledge. The book is well received and is reaching varied individuals. Young adults who are dedicated followers of Jesus Christ are learning to see media, Hollywood and even the world from a Christian perspective, while those who are not necessarily connecting with a church are seeing Jesus in a fresh way. Based on this success, the authors decided to write on Season 2 of LOST, but with a twist: they involved 27 high school juniors and seniors. That, too, was well received, so nineteen students came together for Season 3:

Phil Borel	Pierson Boyer
Tyler Brooks	Pablo Calzada
Brandon Delekta	Ryan Evans
Adam Exelby	Heather Geer
Joshua Gudobba	Charles Hayden, IV
Faith Lieder	Kelsey Lucas
Madison Martin	Josie Murgor
Alexis Nelson	Joshua Peterson
Ericka Seidel	Chas Tenney
Emily Wurm	

LOST Lessons 3 is designed as a "devotional by teens, for teens." This class of nineteen students at Oakland Christian School broke into small groups, watched an episode of LOST, discussed the spiritual implications and then wrote a devotional. Randy Johnson and David Rutledge gave direction and modified the lessons, striving to ensure good Biblical support and a flow that is easier to read. Each lesson begins with a pretty extensive overview of the episode, so someone who has not watched the show can still benefit from the devotional.

Randy Johnson and David Rutledge would like to say a special thank you to Tom Gendich and Rochester Media for believing in youth and publishing LOST Lessons 3, and a thank you to the other professionals who helped:

Laura Hall (http://rebornagain2010.wordpress.com/about-me/) edited the lessons for clarity, spelling and grammar.

Brian Jamieson (http://www.jamiesondesign.net) designed the cover and the book layout.

LOST LESSONS 3
A DEVOTIONAL BY TEENS FOR TEENS

By
Dr. Randy T. Johnson
and
David Rutledge

Table of Contents

1.	Letting Go of the Lies to Face the Truth	1
2.	Deception Hurts	9
3.	Using Words to Encourage	15
4.	"Lean On Me"	23
5.	Tale of Two Brothers	31
6.	Do You?	39
7.	Hate is Murder	47
8.	Life, Liberty, and the Pursuit of Happiness	55
9.	Mark of the Beast	63
10.	The Spirit of Disbelief is Destroyed	73
11.	To Forgive is Divine	81
12.	Seeking Answers	89
13.	When Last is …First	97
14.	The Truth Comes Out	105

15.	Not by Choice, but by Calling	113
16.	Two-Faced	121
17.	Heads I Win, Tails You Lose	129
18.	D.O.H. (Date of Hope)	137
19.	Brigantino	145
20.	"The Blame Game"	153
21.	Count Your Many Blessings	161
22.	To Live To Die	169

About the Authors   177

Caricatures by Don

Oakland Christian School would like to thank Don Pinsent for permission to use his LOST caricatures in this book. Don is a professional artist and fellow believer out of Nova Scotia, Canada.

The image on the next page is the complete composition of 66 characters all together in one mind-blowing image! It is available as prints in two sizes: 11" x 14" for $15 each plus $5 shipping. Or, to appreciate it more fully, order the poster-size (18" x 24") version for $30 each plus $20 shipping! Each one, in either size, comes with a legend indicating all the individual characters.

Don also offers an 11" x 14" of any individual caricature you prefer to have. This costs $15 each plus $5 shipping.

To order a print or contact Don Pinsent, please go to his website: www.CaricaturesbyDon.com

Letting Go of the Lies to Face the Truth | 1

Chapter 1
■ ■ ■

Letting Go of the Lies to Face the Truth

Episode 1
"A Tale of Two Cities"

The episode starts off with a flashback with Jack in his car watching Sarah, his ex-wife, from afar. Jack is struggling to let go of the fact that the divorce is going to go through. Because of this, he lets his overwhelming thoughts take control of who he is and what he believes. In the divorce court, the main question Jack strives to learn is, who is the man that is replacing him in his wife's life? Because of his overwhelming curiosity and stubbornness, he starts to falsify a reality in which he sees his father as the man who took his wife. In doing this, Jack breaks a huge barrier that his father is trying to overcome. Jack's inability to let go led to his father drinking again, after so many months of being sober, as well as Jack's temporary arrest. Sarah receives a call from Jack's drunken father asking her to get Jack out of jail. When Jack gets bailed out, the only thing he asks, "Is that him?" In reply Sarah gives him a bold answer saying, "It doesn't matter who he is, it matters who you're not."

On the island, Jack is locked up in a glass holding cell and is trying to use force to escape. He is taking out all his anger by banging on the glass, trying to force the door open, and by back-talking Juliet. At each attempt that he tries, he fails. Once realizing that a forceful escape is inevitable, he decides to cooperate with Juliet. Juliet, who is trying to calm Jack, shows Jack a record book of his life.

> Juliet: "That was a long time ago. It doesn't matter who we were, it only matters who we are. We know exactly who you are, Jack Shephard."

At the end of the episode, Juliet asks Jack what he would like to know. Going through the flashbacks, Jack's curiosity about the identity of Sarah's lover causes him a lot of pain and causes him to lose himself within. Although it was tough, Jack is finally able to let go and answers Juliet's question by asking if Sarah is happy. At the end of the episode, Jack has matured from the days of his past and is finally able to let go which is an ultimate win for him.

The Bible recounts a major historical event when Peter denies Jesus three times. Mathew's account is found in chapter 26 verses 69-75:

Now Peter was sitting out in the courtyard, and a servant girl came to him. 'You also were with Jesus of Galilee,' she said. But he denied it before them all. 'I don't know what you're talking about,' he said. Then he went out to the gateway, where another servant girl saw him and said to the people there, 'This fellow was with Jesus of Nazareth.' He denied it again, with an oath: 'I don't know the man!' After a little while, those standing there went up to Peter and said, 'Surely you are one of them; your accent gives you away.' Then he began to call down curses, and he swore to them, 'I don't know the man!' Immediately a rooster crowed. Then Peter remembered the word Jesus had spoken: 'Before the rooster crows, you will disown me three times.' And he went outside and wept bitterly.

It took a while for Peter to let go of this mistake, but slowly he began to forgive himself and let God forgive him as well. The next verses display the love of

God and his patience with us. If Peter had kept himself "chained," he would not have experienced God's love and forgiveness

Jesus realized Peter's burden of guilt and approached him in John 21:15-17:

When they had finished eating, Jesus said to Simon Peter, 'Simon son of John, do you love me more than these?' 'Yes, Lord,' he said, 'you know that I love you.' Jesus said, 'Feed my lambs.' Again Jesus said, 'Simon son of John, do you love me?' He answered, 'Yes, Lord, you know that I love you.' Jesus said, 'Take care of my sheep. The third time he said to him, 'Simon son of John, do you love me?' Peter was hurt because Jesus asked him the third time, 'Do you love me?' He said, 'Lord, you know all things; you know that I love you.'

In life, we all have things that we struggle to release. As we can see with Jack, by not letting go, we are held back from the ultimate glory that is in front of us. A wise man once said, "There's no need to miss someone from your past- there's

Sarah: "It doesn't matter who he is. It just matters who you're not".

a reason they didn't make it to your future." Also, as Paul puts it: "Brothers, I do not consider myself yet to have taken hold of it. But one thing I do: Forgetting what is behind and straining toward what is ahead" (Philippians 3:13). However, everything happens for a reason. If we were still with a certain person from the past, there is a great possibility that we would not be where we are now. On the other side, if we would have done something differently, we would not have learned the lesson we were suppose to learn. Everything happens for a reason, so instead of focusing on the "could of's," "should of's," and "would of's," we ought to focus on how we have grown from our past and how our past has set the stage for a brighter future.

Sarah: "Look at the bright side, now you have something to fix."

What are you holding on to, that you need to let go?

_____

_____

_____

_____

What is keeping you from letting go?

_____

_____

_____

_____

Do you believe God is BIG enough to handle everything? If holding on has not worked, why continue?

_____

_____

_____

_____

Picture by Mike Schinkel

"Breathe. Let go, and remind yourself that this is the only one moment you know you have for sure."
-Oprah Winfrey

Chapter 2
■ ■ ■

Deception Hurts

Episode 2
"The Glass Ballerina"

In the opening scene, Sun, as a young girl, breaks a glass ballerina then later blames it on the maid. Back on the island, Sayid, Sun, and Jin are on a sailboat looking for Jack, Sawyer and Kate. Sawyer and Kate are put to work by the others. They are not allowed to talk to each other or anyone otherwise they will be shocked. Sawyer disobeys by kissing Kate and beating up some of the others, only to be shocked and put back to work. There is a flashback to Sun in bed with another man, and he wants to run away to

Sayid to Sun, "What would you know about lying?"

America with her. Sun's father walks in on them. Sun's father sends Jin to "deliver a message" to the man that Sun was in bed with, although Jin is not aware of the situation. At first Jin refuses to deliver the message because he does not want to kill anyone. Sun's father convinces him by saying, "my shame is your shame." Jin delivers the message without killing the man, but demands him to leave the country. Instead, the man jumps off his balcony and dies, with pearls as a gift for Sun, in hand. Back on the island, Sun, Jin, and Sayid build another signal fire to capture some of "the others." Jin and Sayid are waiting on land while Sun is on the boat. Sun gets ambushed, shoots one of the others, and jumps off the boat. Meanwhile, Ben explains to Jack that if he cooperates; he will get to go home.

The story of Samson and Delilah is pretty renowned. Samson falls in love with a woman, Delilah. The Philistines go to Delilah and bribe her to discover the secret to Samson's strength in order to capture him. Delilah asks Samson three times, and each time, Samson tells her lies. When he finally tells her the truth, Samson is betrayed by Delilah and captured by the Philistines. But notice Delilah's response when she discovers

Sayid to Sun, "Lie to Jin for another 20 minutes."

Samson was not being honest: "Delilah then said to Samson, 'Until now, you have been making a fool of me and lying to me. Tell me how you can be tied'" (Judges 16:13). The conversation continues in verse 15: "Then she said to him, 'How can you say, 'I love you,' when you won't confide in me? This is the third time you have made a fool of me and haven't told me the secret of your great strength.'" Both Samson and Delilah were hurt by the other's dishonesty. Samson was physically affected by Delilah's deceit while Delilah was emotionally affected by Samson's deceit. Their story is a perfect example of how both parties in a lie are hurt, no one wins.

The Christian walk should be different. Jesus said in John 14:6 that He is "the way and the truth and the life." Jesus spoke the truth, lived in truth and even is the truth. As followers, we too should strive to walk in truth. Proverbs 19:9 says, "A false witness will not go unpunished, and whoever pours out lies will perish." Sun's lies brought shame and pain. Honesty truly is the best policy.

Do you remember a time when someone deceived you? How did you feel?

Have you ever deceived someone? How do you think they felt?

What consequences can come from deceiving someone?

Picture by Faith Lieder

"With lies you may go ahead in the world, but you can never go back."
-Unknown

Chapter 3
■ ■ ■

Using Words to Encourage

Episode 3
"Further Instructions"

John Locke's journey before and during his adventure on the island is the main focus in episode three. In the previous season, the hatch Locke, Desmond, and Eko were working on exploded. Fortunately, Locke survives the implosion, but his voice is gone. Unable to speak for quite some time, Locke searches for a cure to his speechlessness. In his previous life on as a farmer, Locke frequently spent time in a sweat lodge. A sweat lodge is a secluded area where one can find out their identity and purpose. Locke, seeking to find his purpose, creates a sweat lodge. While in the lodge, Locke sees a vision of Boone pushing him through an airport in a wheelchair. This vision is before the crash, hence the reason why Locke needs the aid of his wheelchair. Boone informs Locke there is someone in danger, and Locke needs to rescue him. Locke, without speaking, attempts to find the person in harm's way,

> "So where are Eko and Desmond?" Charlie asks. "Are they off being mute and building structures as well?"

but Boone reminds him that he will be speechless until he has something worth saying. Boone leaves Locke telling him that "first you have to clean up your own mess." Boone is referring to Locke's lack of faith in Eko. Eko is in danger now because Locke failed to press the button, and now Locke has to fix the mess he created. Locke's vision ends with the image of Eko's bloody walking stick and a ferocious polar bear. Locke emerges from sweat lodge immediately with Charlie waiting eagerly for him. Locke, finally able to use his words, tells Charlie that Eko is in grave danger. Locke and Charlie journey into the jungle to find Eko, and, in the end, the two men save his life.

Locke's story in this episode is similar to a Bible story in Luke. In Luke chapter one, an angel appears to a man named Zacharias. Zacharias and his wife Elizabeth are very old in age, so when an angel reveals to Zacharias that Elizabeth will give birth to a son, he is filled with doubt. Because of his disbelief, Zacharias loses ability to speak until the child is born. Like Locke, Zacharias is speechless until he has something worthwhile to say. This lesson shows that there are consequences for doubting, and Locke and Zacharias both experience this. Locke doubts Eko when Eko tells him to push the button in the hatch, and because of his doubt, Eko is in danger and Locke loses his ability to speak. Zacharias finally speaks up when the child is born. Elizabeth does not know what to name him, and Zacharias says that the child should be named John (who becomes John the Baptist). His speechlessness is released when he finally realizes God's power. He shares the story of his unfaithfulness towards the angel with everyone around him. His heart is truly changed. Zacharias and Lock both realize that words are valuable and things should be thought about before being said.

The tongue, though a seemingly insignificant part of our body, is one of the most powerful and available instruments and can be used to do good and evil. God communicates to use through in words through the Bible, so clearly God has a purpose for the use of words. Words can encourage, exaggerate, witness, deceive, worship, manipulate, communicate, and boast. A single conversation can cut down a person in a second or build him/her up and make his/her day. In the New Testament, James restates this idea. James 3:9-10 says, "With the tongue we praise our Lord and Father, and with it we curse human beings, who have been made in God's likeness. Out of the same mouth come praise and cursing. My brothers and sisters, this should not be." This verse portrays the reality of human nature, praising and cursing with words.

In today's society, people have a tendency to speak before thinking. This is the reason for arguments, bullying, divorce, and war. Using words for evil can be the simplest and deadliest sin. As stated previously, words can change and shape a conversation. Using words to encourage can be better than speaking uselessly. Solomon writes in Ecclesiastes on this same subject. Ecclesiastes 6:11 says, "The more the words, the less the meaning, and how does that profit anyone?" Although there are times to speak up, silence can be meaningful. The famous saying "actions speak louder than words" is true here. Leroy Brownlow captures the thought, "There are times when silence has the loudest voice." Words are important, but, just like salting, use them sparingly to add flavor

> "Hair spray," Charlie says to Locke, "I hate to be the one to point this out to you, but-"

not a disgusting, bitter taste. Overall, understand the power of words and speak good, wise thoughts.

Have you ever said something you wish you could take back? What was it, and how do you feel about it now? Think about your previous mistakes and how you can prevent them in the future.

_____

_____

_____

_____

People say approximately 7,000 to 10,000 words on a daily basis. Do you feel like most of the things you say are worthwhile and have value?

_____

_____

_____

_____

In 1 Thessalonians 5:11, Paul says, "Therefore encourage one another and build each other up, just as in fact you are doing." Challenge yourself to encourage others with your words rather than tearing them down.

_____

_____

_____

_____

Using Words to Encourage | 21

Picture by Yashna M

"Before you speak, think – Is it necessary? Is it true? Is it kind? Will it hurt anyone? Will it improve on the silence?"
– Sri Sathya Sai Baba

Chapter 4
■ ■ ■

Every man for himself

Episode 4
"Lean On Me"

The episode begins with Kate and Sawyer watching the "Others" carry a critically injured Colleen, an "Other" who was shot by Sun the night before, into the station. Sawyer realizes that the injury was inflicted by someone from Oceanic Flight 815. Sawyer then decides to devise a plan to escape. He wants to electrocute Danny, an "Other", using a puddle he created outside his cage with water from his cage. However, Ben Linus, an "Other", hears him over the surveillance system and turns off the electricity prior to him visiting. When Sawyer tries to carry out his plan, Ben knocks him unconscious and has him taken to the

Hydra station. Sawyer wakes up to find himself strapped to a table, where Ben, Tom and two other "Others" watch over him. Sawyer is gagged before the "Others" insert a large needle into his chest. When Sawyer wakes up, Ben is seen carrying a rabbit in a cage; he shakes the cage until the rabbit supposedly dies. Ben proceeds to tell Sawyer he his placed a modified pacemaker inside him. Also, Ben informs him should his heart rate reach 140, his heart would explode. It is at this point, Ben threatens to implant one in Kate if Sawyer tells her what happened to him and that they are watching them inside their cages.

Throughout this episode, Kate and Sawyer stick together and depend on each other as they are both imprisoned and confused. When Sawyer returns to his cage he is apprehensive with Kate's questions. He could even be considered angry with Kate. He even dismisses the idea of escaping when Kate notices she can fit through the bars at the top. Sawyer even warns Kate not to pursue escape. Sawyer knows the terrible consequences if Kate manages to escape and then is captured. So, Sawyer, the best way he can, prevents Kate from the harm she does not know.

In Sawyer's Flashback, his relationship with a fellow inmate shows how one-sided and selfish people can be. He manipulates and uses his supposed "friend" for his own selfish means.

Returning to the present, Kate actually manages to get through the bars in the cage but decides not to escape. Why? Is it because Sawyer said not to? Is it because she was afraid of the unknown? No! Kate doesn't leave because she would be leaving Sawyer behind. Kate knew that if she left Sawyer behind she would be leaving the trust and companionship behind as well. In their cages, Sawyer and Kate form a symbiotic relationship. Sawyer needs Kate just as much as Kate needs Sawyer.

Christians need this sort of relationship just as much. A good example of people sticking together in scripture is David and Jonathan in 1 Samuel 20. In that chapter, the two actually swear friendship, making a pact. They do that so they keep can their friendship alive (now that is a serious friendship!). As a matter of fact, Jonathan loves David just as much as he loves himself (1 Sam. 20:17). As David is ducking and dodging Saul's efforts in killing him, Jonathan, Saul's very own son, takes David under his wing in protecting David from Saul's murderous attempts. After all, David couldn't watch

"Live together, die alone"
–Kate

out for himself forever. He proves this fact to be true in verse three in saying, "Yet as surely as the LORD lives and as you live, there is only a step between me and death." The faithful friend, Jonathan replies to his friend's desperate statement with a humble, "Whatever you want me to do, I'll do for you" (v. 4). In protecting David with all his might, Jonathan is even scorned and sworn upon by his father by siding with the "enemy", David. Without the help of Jonathan, David could have easily been killed, just as Sawyer could have been killed without Kate and vice versa.

Danny, who is the husband of Colleen, goes to Sawyer's cage and violently beats him. The beating stops when Kate tells Danny that she loves Sawyer. Kate cared enough for Sawyer to stop Danny from potentially killing Sawyer. Altogether, Kate will take care of Sawyer and Sawyer will take care of Kate because "Live together, die alone."

As Christians, we need these close companions who truly want the best for us, just like Jonathan wanted the best for David. The Bible speaks of this subject multiple times:

- "A man of many companions may come to ruin, but there is a friend who sticks closer than a brother." Proverbs 18:24

- "Greater love has no one than this, that he lay down his life for his friends." John 15:13

- "A friend loves at all times, and a brother is born for adversity." Proverbs 17:17

- "As iron sharpens iron, so one man sharpens another." Proverbs 27:17

We shouldn't go through hardships or accomplishments in this life alone. It is so simple what we must do for our brothers and sisters in Christ. We must spur each other on in Christ, seeking to make better lives of one another, and ultimately better children of God.

What would you do to protect those you care for? How far would you go in doing so?

Do you have friends that truly want the best for you?

_____

_____

Are you a friend that truly wants the best for your friends?

What can you do to spiritually improve your friend?

Picture by U.S. Embassy New Delhi

"Walking with a friend in the dark is better than walking alone in the light."
– Helen Keller

Chapter 5
■ ■ ■

Tale of Two Brothers

Episode 5
"The Cost of Living"

In a flashback, young Eko tries breaking a lock to get food out of the shed for his brother Yemi. While doing so, he gets caught by a nun from his village. She takes him to the church so he can confess the sins he had committed. He is very stiff to confess, and we never actually see him confess in the show. This event comes back to haunt him years later. Since he has just been injured in the explosion of the hatch and is still unconscious, he has many flashbacks and visions.

The hut in which Eko is recovering catches fire after the vision he has shown his brother with a lighter. This may be the mystical happening of the island or the physical conditions affecting Eko's unconscious state. Yemi tells his brother that he needs to confess in the vision he has. Upon the discovery of the burning building he is carried out of the hut and laid down on the beach. Shortly after Eko is discovered to be missing from where he was laid down. A brief dialogue shows that he has run to a crashed plane in the forest where his brother crashed in a plane. While walking through the jungle, Eko has some scary visions of people he has killed begging for mercy and a small Catholic altar boy asking him if he was a bad man. Eko responds to the small boy by saying, "Only God knows." Upon arriving there, his brother's body is missing. Since there are polar bears on the island, Eko had covered up his brother's body with large rocks so it wouldn't be found.

"I did not ask for the life I was given, but with it I did my best" Eko's confession

After some time his brother begins to lead Eko through the jungle and leads him into a field with red flowers everywhere. His brother proceeds by asking, "Are you ready Eko?" Eko's response is very sarcastic. In his confession, he says he does not need forgiveness because he did only what he needed to do to survive. After that, his bother leads him back into the jungle where the smoke comes out and attacks Eko. Before the smoke attacks, Eko begins to recites the 23rd Psalm. The monster then attacks Eko, beating him wildly against a tree until his body simply cannot take anymore. The smoke recedes into the jungle right before Eko's friends arrive seconds late of saving him.

The imagery of his brother communicating with him throughout the whole episode could have been caused by the powers of the Island and his burdens. In Judges 11, we hear of a warrior named Jephthah. He is sent out of Israel by his brother because he was born of a prostitute. He went to the land of Tob where a gang of scoundrels followed him. Very similarly, Eko joins up with raiders to save his brother from having to go with him, but by doing this, he killed a man. Eko was shunned from the community after that because he was now one of the raiders.

The burden of killing a man to save your brother's life at such a young age must have been tremendous. We don't know much about what else Eko did while he was a part of this gang, but we do know his actions and his lust of power and money caused his brother to die. After his brother died, he took his spot as the father of the church. During this period while he is at the church, he kills three men. The church is boarded up, and he gets angry claiming that it was Yemi's church, and that they couldn't do this. Now on top of all the other things that lead up to his brother's death, which was his fault, the church at which his brother is a priest is now gone because of his actions.

In Isaiah 41:13 it is said, "For I am the LORD, your God, who takes hold of your right hand and says to you, Do not fear. I will help you." What encouraging words in today's world where nothing is stable, and at times we feel alone even though there are six billion other people here. Eko faked being a priest just as I have faked being a Christian for fifteen years of my life. Growing up in the church and going to Christian schools my whole life, I took for granite that I was a Christian. I hadn't stopped and realized that I needed to be a Christian. I didn't see how much I was missing in the wonderful arms of God until I had fallen down to the bottom of the valley and almost gave up the whole game I was playing. But luckily I decided to help out at a middle school retreat that our school hosted and was shown what Christianity truly was and why I truly needed it to survive in this fallen, despairing world. I still struggle with habits and burdens of my past, and I will for a long time to come, but that is no reason why I can't love the Lord. He saved me and loved me which is why the least I can do is worship Him with all that I am and strive to be in his likeness.

Eko gets so close to the salvation and repentance point, but shuns it because he claims all he needs to do is survive. This isn't true. More is to be found in this life than just surviving: God, who is the Creator of the galaxies which includes you and every atom of your structure. He knows exactly where you are and why.

What burdens have you been keeping that have made life difficult to live from day to day?

_____

_____

_____

_____

Have you considered giving your burdens to God like it says in Matthew 11:28, "Come to me, all you who are weary and burdened, and I will give you rest"?

_____

_____

What is preventing you from giving these burdens to God?

Picture by Chas Tenney

"The key to change... is to let go of fear."
– Rosanne Cash

Chapter 6

■ ■ ■

Do You?

Episode 6
"I Do"

In flashbacks, we see that Kate, who is currently going by the name Monica, is in an ironic relationship with a police officer and is planning to marry him the next day. During their wedding, the preacher ironically says, "When I first met you Kate, I was struck by your honesty," and that, "what you see is what you get." Sometime after the wedding, Kate calls the Marshal who has been hunting her for her crimes and tells him that she does not want to run anymore. The Marshal guesses that she is with a man, and says that if she can settle down and stay put, he will stop chasing her. Right before Kate hangs up in order to avoid being tracked, he ends the conversation with, "But you and I both know that's not gonna happen." He ends up being right. After Kate finds out she is not pregnant, she drugs her husband so he will not remember her confession of who she is, and leaves.

While on the island with "The Others," Jack examines the x-rays of Ben's tumor and tells him that he should have been in surgery yesterday - the tumor is borderline inoperable. Ben then tells Jack that he can have whatever he needs to do the surgery. Jack responds coldly, "I didn't say I was gonna do it. I just wanted you to understand how you're gonna die." This leads to Juliet making a deal with Kate to try and convince Jack to do the surgery. If she does not try to convince Jack to save Ben, Pickett (Kate and Sawyer's jailor) is going to kill Sawyer. Kate and Jack are reunited, only for Kate to beg Jack to do the surgery in order to save Sawyer's life. Jack refuses at first, but after escaping and seeing Kate and Sawyer together in their cage, he decides to perform the surgery. While in the middle of the surgery, Jack makes an incision in Ben's kidney and says that if Kate and Sawyer are not released and safe in an hour, he will not stitch Ben's cut and, consequently, he will die.

"Close your eyes freckles."

Throughout the episode, we see that Kate has always struggled with who she is. She is always going by a false name and can never stay in one place for any length of time. She is essentially living a lie. This is similar to the story, in Genesis 27 of Jacob and Esau, where Jacob pretends to be Esau in order to receive his father Isaac's blessing.

Jacob and Esau were twins, with Esau being the older of the two. Following Jewish tradition, Esau should receive his father's blessing when his father died. However, Isaac's wife, Rebekah, favors Jacob more than Esau and would rather have him receive the blessing. Consequently, she devises a devious plot to make that a reality when she overhears a blind and dying Isaac's request for Esau to make his favorite goat meal in preparation for passing on his blessing.

Rebekah's plan is that, while Esau is out hunting, she will prepare the goat meal, Jacob will put the goat's fur on his arms and neck (since Esau was very hairy) and wear Esau's best clothes, and then pretend to be Esau. The plan unfolds, and it seems as if Jacob was going to be caught in his lie when Isaac pointed out that it sounds like Jacob instead of Esau. However, after feeling the

> Saint Monica was the mother of Augustine, who wrote "Confessions."

fur, tasting the food, and hearing Jacob's lie that he is, in fact, Esau, Isaac bestows his blessing on Jacob. Soon after Jacob leaves, Esau enters the tent and asks for his blessing. Isaac has to break the news to him that he only has one blessing to give, and that it has already been bestowed onto Jacob. Jacob's lie about his identity worked.

Jacob isn't the only person to ever pretend to be someone he was not. We may not pretend to be our brother, but at times we do pretend to be someone we are not. We pretend to be a person that other people will like, or the person that will make us more popular. We need to realize that people who like us for who we pretend to be are not really worth it. It is the people who like you just the way you are that are worth being around. So avoid these identity crises by asking yourself a very hard question: Who am I?

Describe yourself in a few words

Are there times when you would say you aren't yourself? If so, why?

We also see that Kate tells lies on a regular basis - so much so that she has gotten good enough to seem like an honest person. We know that lying is a sin. It says so in the Ten Commandments: "You shall not give false testimony against your neighbor." Lying not only affects the person being lied to, but also the liar. It could forever affect your relationship with that person and the trust between the two of you.

Trust is very hard to earn, but very easy to destroy. It takes many actions to earn somebody's trust, but one lie can destroy it and send you back to square one. The saying, "Honesty is the best policy," may be a bit cliché, but it is a more accurate statement than we realize. There are times where we think, "I just can't tell them the truth. It would only make things worse." While the truth may be bad, it is better than the other person thinking everything is fine when, in reality, the truth is something totally different. Telling the truth will also leave you feeling free, instead of having a lie in your past eat away at you. As John 8:32 says, "Then you will know the truth, and the truth will set you free." Coming clean is better than hiding your dirt.

Saint Monica's patronage: those who have difficult marriages.

What are some reasons for lying to someone?

_____

_____

_____

_____

How would telling the truth change the outcome compared to lying?

_____

_____

_____

_____

How can you rebuild your trust, or how can someone earn your trust after they lied?

_____

_____

_____

_____

Picture by Chas Tenney

"A lie has speed, but truth has endurance."
–Edgar J. Mohn

Chapter 7

■ ■ ■

Hate is Murder

Episode 7
"Not in Portland"

Juliet has a meeting with Richard about moving her research out to Portland. She reluctantly refuses, claiming that her ex-husband would never let her go. While explaining to Richard why her husband will not let her go, Juliet becomes flustered and says that the only way he would allow her to leave would be if he got hit by a bus. Near the end of the episode, Juliet returns to work to tell her ex-husband that her independent research on her sister has worked. While Juliet tells him he begins to walk out into the street, where he pauses for a moment, upon which he is promptly hit by a bus.

In Matthew 5, Jesus begins to preach his famous "Sermon on the Mount." This sermon is comprised of many miniature sermons instructing people on how to live to glorify God. Most of Jesus' instructions have to do with love; however, in verses 21 and 22, Jesus begins to talk about "anger without reason" or "hate." He warns against such things saying,

> You have heard that it was said to the people long ago, 'You shall not murder, and anyone who murders will be subject to judgment.' But I tell you that anyone who is angry with a brother or sister will be subject to judgment. Again, anyone who says to a brother or sister, 'Raca,' is answerable to the court. And anyone who says, 'You fool!' will be in danger of the fire of hell

While in a fluster, Juliet was telling Richard her life would in some small way be easier if only her ex-husband was hit by a bus before she could even think of what she was saying. She showed her true feelings about her husband, and even though he is portrayed as a jerk in this episode, her feelings were still shameful when she admitted them out loud.

> "Don't get mad at me, just because you were dumb enough to fall for the whole Wookie prisoner gag." - Sawyer

It is not easy to find someone who wants to believe that on the inside she can have wishes drastic enough to wish someone else was dead. However, every human being is capable of extremely evil things because of our sinful nature. In Isaiah 64:6, Isaiah calls out to God saying,

> "All of us have become like one who is unclean,
>   and all our righteous acts are like filthy rags;
> we all shrivel up like a leaf,
>   and like the wind our sins sweep us away."

Isaiah says this because he realizes that no one is perfect - every person is capable of evil. No one is above hate, and, according to Jesus, hate is no different than murder.

Often we may find ourselves justifying our sins, even sins like hate. If you were to ask any group of people who know about the horrors that went on in Nazi concentration camps during World War II what they thought about Hitler, the response would probably be anything but positive. If people were given the chance to kill Hitler, would they take it if he was still operating concentration camps today? We may be surprised on how many people would say yes because they believe it will help other people. However, Christ talks about the way that Christians should treat their enemies in Mathew 5:44 saying, "But I tell you, love your enemies and pray for those who persecute you." According to Christ, we should love our enemies and even "bless" them. That is, we should make an effort to "do well" to them, and even if they are the most evil people in the world; we should still treat them with love. We are capable of everything they are capable of, and any amount of hate, which in its most basic form is just the absence of love, is just the same as murder. Even though they may deserve it is not a justifiable action, because if we are honest with ourselves, we will find that no one deserves life or love, yet Christ gives both to everyone freely and unconditionally.

In Mathew 5:44 Jesus tells his followers to love people no matter what they do and no matter who they are. He not only instructs His followers to love them, but He also tells them how to love by saying that we are to "bless them that curse you" and "do good to them that hate you." Living a life of love is no easy task. Often we are caught up in believing that someone deserves our hate because of how evil they are, but Christ, being the ultimate example, lived a life of love. He was never cruel to anyone, and he treated everyone as an equal (even treating his disciples above himself by washing their feet when he was their master), with love and respect.

In reading this devotional about hate, did someone's name come to your mind?

_____

_____

_____

_____

Are you willing to follow Jesus and forgive them?

_____

_____

_____

_____

How could you take the huge step and bless them?

_____

_____

_____

_____

Picture by Paolo Massa

"We have just enough religion to make us hate, but not enough to make us love one another."
- Jonathan Swift

Chapter 8
■ ■ ■

Life, Liberty, and the Pursuit of Happiness

Episode 8
"Flashes Before Your Eyes"

    The episode starts off with a timer reaching zero. Desmond tears through the bookshelf to find the key to the fail safe mechanism. He turns the key, and his whole life flashes before his eyes. He wakes up on the floor in his apartment with red paint all over him. He was painting and had fallen off the ladder on the ground in his apartment. His girlfriend, Penny, walks over to him and checks to make sure he is okay. Desmond is confused but happy, and says that he is fine. Later on, while Desmond is walking out of Widmore Industries, the company at which Penny's father works, he sees Charlie playing the guitar on the street for money.

He immediately recognizes him, but Charlie does not recognize him. At that point Desmond has a mini instance of déjà vu and realizes that he has lived all this before. He goes to meet his friend Donovan, a physicist, at a pub to ask him about time travel. Donovan basically laughs at him and tells him that he is crazy.

Later on, Desmond walks into a jewelry store looking to buy a ring to propose to Penny. The lady who is working there suggests a ring for him that is nice, but not expensive. Desmond immediately loves it and asks to buy it. The woman says that he cannot buy the ring. Desmond is taken back by this and is confused. The woman says that he does not buy the ring; in fact, he does not even marry Penny. She says if he buys the ring, "[he] will kill all of us." She decides to take Desmond out to further convince him of what she is talking about. While they are out, the woman points out a man wearing bright red Converse shoes. She says that it is a rather different fashion statement. Later on, the man with the bright red shoes was crushed by a cement wall falling on him close to Desmond and the woman. Desmond immediately knew that the woman was aware that this was going to happen, yet she did nothing to stop it. She said that it would not have mattered, and if she would have told the man of this to save him, the next day he would have been killed. And if she told him about the next day as well, he would have died of something else down the road. She said that there was no way of stopping this cycle and that the universe will "course correct" itself to kill him a different way. Later on in the episode, since Desmond can see how people die before they do, he ends up saving Charlie from drowning and getting struck by lightning. He knows that he cannot keep saving him, but he wants to try as hard as he can to prevent his death.

Desmond basically went out of his way to save Charlie multiple times. Charlie has done nothing to him to make him act like this. Desmond's actions are similar to the Good Samaritan in Luke 10. In verses 30-35, the story is about a man who is attacked by robbers and is left half dead on the side of the road. Both a priest and a Levite pass the man without helping him because of their own selfish reasons. The priest and Levite are similar to the woman at the jewelry store. Just like these two characters from the Bible who leave the man to die, the woman let the man with red shoes die without trying to save him. In Luke 10, a third man comes by who is a Samaritan

"That guy, he sees the future, Dude" – Hurley

and saves the half-dead man. The Samaritan had no reason to save him. The man had done nothing to the Samaritan; he just wanted to keep him alive. This is also what Desmond did.

This is a tough situation for most humans, because by nature we are selfish people. Most people have a, "if it does not affect me, not my problem" type of mentality. In both the account of the Good Samaritan and the LOST episode, Desmond and the Samaritan go out of their way to help those in need. Desmond helped Charlie who had nothing to do with him. It did not affect him, but he still saved him. To what extent would you go to save someone?

This question ultimately comes down to the person and his morals, however, I believe that if you can help someone in need, then you must help them, no matter the situation. Think of it this way: if you were in need or in trouble and someone else knew about it, wouldn't you want that person to help you no matter what? This goes back to, "do unto others as they would do unto you." Desmond shows this in the episode by helping and saving Charlie. Desmond felt inclined to save him.

A key aspect of this episode of LOST is whether or not people have the ability to change the future through kindness. The woman from the jewelry store says in the episode that you cannot change the person's future by saving them from their death. Even if you save them once, it will not change the overall future for them. In the episode, I feel that Desmond does not really agree with this. This is why he keeps helping Charlie. I think that in life, you can change the future by saving people. If you save them, you change how, what or when things happen.

To what extent would you go to save someone?

_____

_____

_____

_____

Are you inclined to help someone if you can?

_____

_____

_____

Can you change the future by helping someone?

Who should you help right now?

Picture by David Woo

"It is more blessed to give than to receive"
—Acts 20:35

Chapter 9
■ ■ ■

Mark of the Beast

Episode 9
"Stranger in a Strange Land"

In the beginning of the episode, Tom comes into the room where Jack is staying and says that they are moving him. As they leave, he notices that Juliet is handcuffed and being taken into his room. He asks why, but all they tell him is that she is in trouble. Later that night, Juliet comes out to ask Jack if he will help with Ben because his stitches have become infected. He refuses to help. Another woman comes out and says she needs to ask Jack some questions. She also notices his tattoo, and asks if he knows what it means. He says yes, with a tone meaning: drop it; I do not want to talk about it anymore. She questions him on Juliet, but he does not answer it fully and asks to be taken back to his cage.

Later Jack remembers how he was vacationing right before they landed on the island. He went out one morning, and he decided that he was going to build a kite and fly it. He struggled at first, but a nice young, attractive woman comes up to him to help him out. They get the kite built, and then they fly it together happily. Afterwards, this woman takes Jack out to a local restaurant where they sit, and have a nice breakfast together. She tells him that she has a special gift, but he is not allowed to know what it is. Jack leaves it alone not showing much interest in it, or looking too far into it.

> Tom: "You see this glass house you're living in, Jack? How about I get you some stones?"

They enjoy each other's conversation, and they continue to see each other. As the weeks progress, the two grow more and more fond of each other. She shows up late one night at where he is saying, and he casual asks where she was. She says that she was just working, and it is not important. This time it really gets to him, and he becomes curious as to what she does that is so important he cannot tell her.

Late one night, Jack follows her down an alley and into a room he did not recognize. At first glance he

Mark of the Beast

assumes that it is just a tattoo parlor, so he asks her why the big secret. She tells him that it is not a tattoo parlor, and her gift is more than he thinks. Her gift is that she is able to see who people really are. She marks her people with what they really are. Jack asks what he is, but she does not want to tell him. She finally tells him that he is a great and strong leader, and that he will do great things. He tells her to mark him, but she does not want to because it is against her people. He forces her to do it, but she tells him there will be consequences. He says that there always are. The following morning multiple men surround Jack, noticed that he has been marked and beat him. They tell him to leave and to never come back.

Finishing the episode, Ben's daughter, Alex, comes to Jack's cage and tells him that Juliet is in trouble - they are going to kill her. He asks if her dad is still in charge. She tells him yes, and she gets him out of the cage. They immediately go to Ben where he is still immobile from the surgery. Jack tells him he will help him as long as Juliet is pardoned and saved. He agrees and Jack saves her, but they said they were going to mark her. The next morning Juliet

> Sawyer: "You have backyards? Well ain't that quaint."

brings Jack food, and she thanks him. He asks her so show the mark, and she does, revealing that it is a star-like shape, but it is quite red. He gets an aloe leaf, and rubs it on it to make it feel better. Jack is taken now with Ben to help out with his infection. While leaving the woman who asked him questions tells him that his marks do not mean what he thinks they do. She says they mean, "He walks among us, but he is not one of us."

The Bible story that can most closely be related to this episode would have to be Samson and Delilah. These verses are found throughout the chapters of Judges 14-16. Samson thinks he has it good by being able to be with Delilah, even though he knows that she is a Philistine. He believes that besides that she is great to him. She is beautiful, nice, and takes care of him. She loves his strength, and she wants to know how he got it. He says he cannot tell her. This is exactly like between Jack and the woman on his vacation. Delilah keeps pushing on where his strength comes from until he finally tells her that it is his hair. He cuts it off during his sleep, and so he loses all of his strength. He is chained to two

Jack: "I'd like to go back to my cage now."

great pillars in the middle of the Philistine House. The Philistines were doing evil things and praying to gods during this time he was chained. He prayed to God to give him his strength one last time. He did, and Samson brought down the whole House, taking him and all the Philistines there with him.

Proverbs 3:5 is a common verse used to remind us how we should respond: "Trust in the LORD with all your heart and lean not on your own understanding." A less common verse that gives the same challenge is Jeremiah 17:7, "But blessed is the man who trusts in the LORD, whose confidence is in him." We need to trust in the Lord. He is our salvation. Isaiah 26:4 is such a strong proclamation, "Trust in the LORD forever, for the LORD, the LORD, is the Rock eternal."

Using this episode of Lost, one has to think very deeply on things. Great thinking is required when it comes to trust. It is not always easy to be able to trust someone, not knowing them fully. Honesty is always the best policy. That is why you must ask yourself:

What do you put your trust in?

_____

_____

_____

_____

People are different in many different ways. No one is exactly the same. No one has the same talents or gifts given by God. You have to use these gifts that He gives you very wisely. They are not toys, and must not be misused or taken advantage of. Ask yourself:

What are your gifts?

_____

_____

_____

_____

How do you use your gift(s)?

_____

_____

_____

_____

Lastly, everyone is given their own mark that people looked upon them with. This mark is going to be with you where ever you go. You want people to think of the right things of you what is on the inside not necessarily on the outside. After the woman told Jack what his tattoo said, he turned to her and said, "That's what is says, that's not what it means." That why you have to ask:

What would be your mark you carry with you?

_____

_____

_____

_____

Picture by Stephen Klein

"Trust, but verify."
–Ronald Reagan

The Spirit of Disbelief is Destroyed

Chapter 10

■ ■ ■

The Spirit of Disbelief is Destroyed

Episode 10
"Tricia Tanaka is Dead"

The episode begins with a flashback from Hurley's life. He is trying to fix an old car, when his father tells him to just go ahead and try to start it. Young Hurley knows it will not start but goes ahead and obeys his father. The broken car does not start. At this point, Hurley's father tells him the Hurley needs to believe good things will happen, because then they will. A moment later, Hurley's father leaves on a bike, and gives Young Hurley a candy bar. The rest of the flash back scenes take place during Hurley's adulthood.

> **Hurley:** "Mr. Clucks got hit by a meteor, or an asteroid, I don't know the difference, but it's gone."

He is standing in front of a restaurant he has just purchased after winning the lottery. Nothing has been fairing well for him. Everything he has gotten involved with or purchased with his money seems to go wrong. As Hurley is talking with the reporter Tricia Tanaka, a meteor crashes into his new restaurant. In the process the reporter, Tricia Tanaka, is killed. Hurley returns home determined to rid himself of a curse, he believes is upon him. The numbers he chose for the lottery are connected with his curse and he is adamant on going to Australia. Once there, he might find some answers. His mother tries to dissuade him but to no avail. So, she reveals to him that his father

> Charlie: "Yeah, chase the dog with the skeletal arm into the creepy jungle. You be my guest."

is back in town after being gone for most of Hurley's life. Hurley's father cannot establish a connection with him so he finally admits he is just here for the money. Yet, he also wants a real relationship with Hurley. Hurley sets off to Australia, determined to give all his new money away.

On the Island, Hurley starts off by telling the deceased Libby most of the recent events on the Island. Hurley then learns that Desmond believes Charlie will die, eventually. All this is running through Hurley and

The Spirit of Disbelief is Destroyed | 75

Charlie's heads when the dog, Vincent, approaches them with a dead man's arm. Hurley runs after the dog and runs into an old abandoned van. Hurley runs back to camp to recruit some help to get the van going. Only Jin volunteers to help Hurley and Sawyer gets sucked to into helping them. Once they are back at the van, they find beer and maps. They prop the van up and Hurley looks for Charlie. He tells him they should start the van and make their own luck. They ride the van down a hill and almost die. But, at the last possible moment, the van starts and Charlie and Hurley survive. Back at camp all do nice things for their ladies. Sawyer cannot seem to find Kate. Kate has gone to recruit Locke and Sayid in order to go find Jack. On their way they are joined by Rousseau, Alex's mother, and the episode is set up for the next one.

In the Bible there is a story of a man who refused to believe something God told him. He did not have the faith to believe God would or could keep his promise. Luke 1:8-13 reveals how Zechariah's prayer request is answered and he doubts it. Verses 18-20 contain the story.

> David Reyes:"In this world, son, you've got make your own luck."

Once when Zechariah's division was on duty and he was serving as priest before God, he was chosen by lot, according to the custom of the priesthood, to go into the temple of the Lord and burn incense. And when the time for the burning of incense came, all the assembled worshipers were praying outside. Then an angel of the Lord appeared to him, standing at the right side of the altar of incense. When Zechariah saw him, he was startled and was gripped with fear. But the angel said to him: 'Do not be afraid, Zechariah; your prayer has been heard. Your wife Elizabeth will bear you a son, and you are to call him John.'

Verses 18-20 describe the consequences of his lack of faith:

Zechariah asked the angel, 'How can I be sure of this? I am an old man and my wife is well along in years.' The angel said to him, 'I am Gabriel. I stand in the presence of God, and I have been sent to speak to you and to tell you this good news. And now you will be silent and not able to speak until the day this happens, because you did not believe my words, which will come true at their appointed time.'

Zachariah did not believe and because of that he was silenced. In our lives we should never doubt the Word of God. When He speaks we should listen.

The Spirit of Disbelief is Destroyed

A wise man once said, "Faith consists in believing when it is beyond the power of reason to believe". Unlike Zachariah, we shouldn't have doubts when it comes to what God tells us. Proverbs tells us to trust in the Lord with all our hearts and lean not on our own understanding (3:5). In faith we put our trust in God and follow His word. Because of this, our relationship grows in God and we are able to accomplish all tasks through God's help. Being sons and daughters of God has its benefits because with God in us nothing can be against. However, in order for this to be true we must believe in him.

What is something you believe God wants you to do?

_____

_____

_____

Do you believe you can accomplish God's will?

_____

_____

Is there anything in life that causes you to doubt yourself? If so what is it?

What is your strongest belief in?

The Spirit of Disbelief is Destroyed

Picture by R'eyes

"We are what we believe we are "
– C.S. Lewis

Chapter 11
■ ■ ■

To Forgive is Divine

Episode 11
"Enter 77"

In this episode, Kate, Locke, and Sayid set off into the jungle to rescue Jack. They find a farmhouse, and a man with an eye patch lives there. Kate, Locke, and Sayid go into the house, and the man tells them his name is Mikhail, and he was the last living member of the Dharma Initiative. Mikhail informs them of the war against the hostiles. Sayid figures out that the man is not a part of Dharma and is in fact, one of the "Others." After a struggle, Kate and Sayid tie Mikhail up. In the meantime, Locke is attempting to beat a chess game on the computer.

> "Computers don't cheat. That's what makes being human so distinctly wonderful." – Locke

The flashbacks go back to

Sayid working as a chef in a restaurant. A man named Sammy asks Sayid to come look at his restaurant to see if he would be interested in working there. Upon arriving to the restaurant, Sammy and his men attack Sayid and knock him out. Sayid is then chained up and tortured in a back room of the restaurant. Sammy accuses Sayid of torturing his wife when he was in the National Guard. Sayid continually claims that he does not know the woman. Sammy's wife comes to talk to him alone. She tells him a story about her cat that was previously abused by some children and she rescued him. She tells Sayid that he is the one who makes her constantly feel unsafe like the cat. Sayid admits that he tortured her and that her face haunts him every day. He apologizes for what he did and Sammy's wife forgives him and lets him go free.

> Hurley: "Look, Dude, all I know is the sky turned purple. After that I don't ask questions. I just make myself a salad and move on."

Back on the beach, Hurley makes a ping pong table and plays against Sawyer. Kate and Sayid find the basement of the house, which is rigged with C4 explosives. Locke wins the computer game and the Dharma instructor comes on the screen. Through a series of steps given by the instructor, Locke enters "77." When they are leaving with Mikhail as a prisoner,

To Forgive is Divine

the house blows up.

This episode has a strong and clear theme: forgiveness. Pay close attention to this certain instruction, "Has there been an incursion on this station by the Hostiles? If so, enter 77." Basically, if the enemy attacks, enter 77. In Matthew 18:15-20, Jesus gives instructions about what to do when someone has sinned against you:

> If your brother sins against you, go and show him his fault, just between the two of you. If he listens to you, you have won your brother over. But if he will not listen, take one or two others along, so that 'every matter may be established by the testimony of two or three witnesses.' If he refuses to listen to them, tell it to the church; and if he refuses to listen even to the church, treat him as you would a pagan or a tax collector.

After Jesus says this, Peter speaks up and asks how many times he should forgive his brother who has sinned against him. Should he forgive him seven times? Jesus answers, "I tell you, not seven times, but seventy-seven times" (Matthew 18:22). The writers of Lost must have been thinking of this passage –

Sun: "No nicknames. If you lose, no nicknames for anyone for a week."

seventy-seven times does relate to enter 77. It seems simple enough, but do we always forgive so easily?

In the parable of the unmerciful servant, a man is unable to pay off a debt owed to his master. The master orders that the man's wife, children, and all other belongings be sold to pay the debt. The man begs for more time, promising to pay off the debt, and the master grants it. Most commentaries agree this would be equal to millions of dollars. When the man is approached by a fellow servant who is indebted to him, he shows no mercy and throws the fellow servant in prison. The debt was a few pennies in comparison. Even though the man was forgiven a great deal, he refuses to forgive someone else even a little. When the master finds out about it, he turns the man over to the jailors to be tortured until he pays off all of his debt. Like the unmerciful servant, when we do not forgive we will be punished by our heavenly Father.

Is there anyone that you need to forgive?

_____

_____

How do you feel when someone forgives you?

David says, "You are forgiving and good, O Lord, abounding in love to all who call to you" (Psalm 86:5). Therefore, God will forgive us; we just have to ask Him. Paul wrote, "But you were washed, you were sanctified, you were justified in the name of the Lord Jesus Christ and by the Spirit of our God" (1 Corinthians 6:11). Because Jesus died on the cross for our sins, we are sanctified and washed clean of those sins. Even though God will forgive us, that does not mean that we can do whatever we please and ask God for forgiveness later. As Christians we should strive to be more like Christ so that asking for forgiveness should be sincere and true in our hearts.

How do you feel knowing that God forgives us no matter what?

_____

_____

_____

What are you going to do now that you know God will forgive you?

_____

_____

_____

_____

To Forgive is Divine

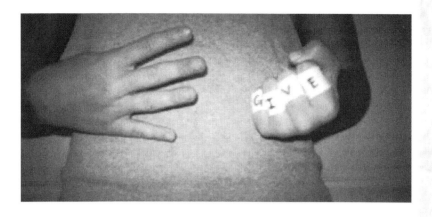

Picture by Faith Lieder

Good nature and good sense must ever join; to err is human, to forgive divine."
– Alexander Pope

Chapter 12

■ ■ ■

Seeking Answers

Episode 12
"Par Avion"

Claire's testimony is told in episode twelve. With flashbacks including a tragic car accident and her mother's unfortunate death, Claire's behavior and tendency to try and manage things in her own hands is revealed. Early in the episode, Claire finds a flock of tagged seagulls. Excited about the possibility to be rescued from the island, Claire goes to all costs to try and catch a seagull. Charlie and Desmond, though, prevent her from doing so. According to Desmond's psychic visions, Charlie will die attempting to help Claire, so the two do everything to ruin Claire's plan. Claire becomes upset, and, again, tries to manage issues herself. She secretly follows Desmond one day out to the bluff, and when he catches a nesting seagull, Claire begins to question him on Charlie and his quirky behavior. Desmond explains the whole thing, filling Claire in on Charlie's supposed death.

Also, in this episode, Locke, Sayid, and Kate are still on the hunt for the "Others." Using the electrical map they found in the station, they discover where the "others" live and realize that what they thought was Jack's imprisonment is actually an agreement made between him and the "others."

A story in the Old Testament between Joshua and the Gibeonites is just like Claire's story. In Joshua 9, the Gibeonites come into an Israelite town pretending to be ambassadors from afar wishing to make a covenant, or promise, with the Israelites not to wage war against them. Joshua is deceived by their tattered clothes, old wineskins, dried out bread, and their twisted lies, and he falls into their trap. Joshua and the Israelites believe them, and, without going to God for direction, sign a peace treaty promising not to hurt their people. Three days later, Joshua discovers the truth. He is embarrassed and ashamed that he did not trust or go to God. As an effect, the Israelite nation is unable

> "I woke up this morning and decided it was time to stop feeling sorry for myself and seize the day. And I can't think of anyone I'd rather do some day seizing with than you. So? What do you say? Let's drop the cherub off with Auntie Sun and Uncle Jin, and you and I will go for a little stroll."

to defeat the Gibeonites. The Lord is disappointed in Joshua's leadership, and He has to punish the Israelites for Joshua's mistake.

Just like Joshua, Claire takes things into her own hands. She distrusts people on the island, and she fails to ask for advice or help. Instead, her actions result in anger, stress, and confusion just like with Charlie and Desmond.  She becomes too overwhelmed with Charlie's sadness and searches for her own answers without seeking outside help. Because she is unable to trust Charlie and Desmond, Claire is hurt through their behavior and words, just like the Israelites were in the Old Testament.

When our set plays go awry, we tend to think, "God has forsaken us." People nowadays struggle to submit their whole lives to the Lord. Instead, each person clings onto his life, his way, and his future so tightly that nothing could rip them apart. We tend to forget the verse, Jeremiah 29:11, "'For I know the plans I have for you,' declares the LORD, 'plans to prosper you and not to harm you, plans to give you a hope and a future." God is so good. He is our Creator and our biggest fan. He is our daily organizer, and His plan is far greater than anything we could ever patch together. We just have to take the next step and trust. In this episode, Claire struggles to trust in something or someone greater than herself. So, instead of having a stress-free lifestyle, Claire is pounded with one issue after another, and she is too prideful to ask for help. As Christ's followers, we sometimes tend to lift our open hands to God and trust. A verse in Proverbs tells us to do just this. Proverbs 3:5-6 states, "Trust in the Lord with all your heart and lean not on your own understanding; in all your way submit to him, and he will make your paths straight." When we give God the steering wheel, things change for the better immediately. Although hardships will come, trusting in God can lighten those burdens. God has laid ahead the perfect path for us, all we have to do is take the first step.

"No," Locke says, "I like dogs."

Who do you talk to when searching for answers? Do you talk to anyone at all? We can talk to God anytime, anywhere through prayer and worship. Talking to friends, parents, or mentors can be helpful too.

Do you trust that God has a plan for your future? Even in the midst of challenging times? Think about all the wonderful adventures God has in store for you, and then ask yourself if you are willing to take them.

Challenge yourself to keep a prayer diary or journal. Notice how God answers your prayers and works in your life. God is good, and He has a plan for everything. Over time, your journal will be filled with proof of God's existence through the miracles exhibited in your life.

Picture by Hobvious Sudoneighm

"If we value the pursuit of knowledge, we must be free to follow wherever that search may lead us. The free mind is not a barking dog to be tethered on a ten-foot chain."
– Adalai Stevenson

Chapter 13
■ ■ ■

When Last is ...First

Episode 13
"The Man from Tallahassee"

This episode is primarily centered on Locke. We find out about Locke's past and more on the origin of his disability. Before getting on the island, Locke was cheated out of a kidney by his father. This symbolized a betrayal of trust with his father, and we begin to understand more about the moral character of Locke's father and Locke's relationship with him. Later, we find out that Locke's father has been scamming women out of their money. When Locke confronts his father at his house, his father lunges at him, and catapults Locke out of a window. Locke falls eight stories; he survives but is disabled. After the incident, Locke became emotionally distant and had little self-worth. Back on

> "You fell eight stories and didn't die. Don't tell me what you can't do."
> —Ben

the island, Locke, Kate, Sayid, and Rousseau are attempting to rescue Jack. Kate and Sayid are captured by the "Others." When Kate is asked if there is anyone else with them, she replies that it is just the two. Later we find Ben being woken up by Locke at gunpoint. Locke begins to threaten Ben about the whereabouts of the submarine. This submarine is used by the "Others" to get on and off the island. Then Ben and Locke proceed to have a conversation. During this conversation, Ben asks Locke to imagine a "very, very large box" that can create anything a person desires. Later, Ben escorts Locke to a hallway with the very "magical" box. When the "magical" box was opened, it turned out to be Locke's father. Locke, completely astounded by this revelation, has only one word, "Dad?"

Nehemiah is a good example of how God uses people of a "lower" position in the world's eyes. Nehemiah, simply a cup bearer, fulfilled the extraordinary task of rebuilding the walls of Jerusalem. In fact, Nehemiah and some men completed a mission that should have taken many years to do, and they accomplished it in only 52 days. This scenario can be seen with Ben and Locke. Locke destroyed the submarine. Not even Ben himself could have completed the task Locke performed. In Nehemiah's case, this goes to show that God can use anybody, no matter what the position, to do anything if he knows that the motives align with the will of God. In a way, Locke's motives matched with Ben's motives and they accomplished the task of destroying the submarine. Nehemiah 6:15-16 explains, "So the wall was completed on the twenty-fifth of Elul, in fifty-two days. When all our enemies heard about this, all the surrounding nations were afraid and lost their self-confidence, because they realized that this work had been done with the help of our God."

Even Jesus chose people of low position to walk by his side when he chose the disciples. In Lost, Ben used Locke, an average person, to complete a significant task for him. Jesus  didn't choose people of royalty as disciples, but rather tax collectors, regular people like Levi/Matthew (Mark 2:13).The episode shows how difficult it is for Locke when he is placed in his wheel chair, as it puts him in a lower position. Sometimes, this is how the world deals with people. We fail to realize that God is great at using ordinary people of this earth, people who society may consider worthless. God does not see earthly positions as humans do. The Bible gives a good example of that in Matthew "So the last will be first, and the first will be last" (Matthew 20:16).

> Ben: "We have two giant hamsters running in a large wheel at our secret underground lair."

How are you being used by God today?

_____

_____

_____

_____

Do you believe God can, and is using you?

_____

_____

_____

_____

Do you have the willing heart for God to use you?

If so, what are some ways God could use you for his glory even more?

Can you pray to be used by God?

last

"Do you wish to be great? Then begin by being. Do you desire to construct a vast and lofty fabric? Think first about the foundations of humility. The higher your structure is to be, the deeper must be its foundation."-
– St. Augustine

Chapter 14

■ ■ ■

The Truth Comes Out

Episode 14
"Exposé"

The episode starts out with Nikki running through the jungle and burying something in the dirt. She then stumbles into the clearing where Sawyer and Hurley are playing ping pong and are witnesses to her collapse. They immediately rush over to see what's wrong, but Nikki can only utter something barely audible before dying. A flashback shows that Nikki was a star on a popular TV show called Expose' and also had an affair with the director, Howard Zukerman. After Paulo and Nikki poison Howard, they steal his key to unlock a safe with a Matryoshka doll that Howard has hidden diamonds worth $8,000,000. A later flashback shows that Paulo and Nikki boarded Oceanic Flight 815 with

> Hurley: "No offense, Dude, but as far as superpowers go, yours is kind of lame."

the diamonds, and, after the crash, they both set out to find them. Paulo finds the diamonds and his nicotine gum (to help his addiction to smoking) at the bottom of a lake, but informs Nikki that he did not find anything. He then hides the diamonds in the Pearle Station's toilet for safe keeping. We all see that Dr. Arzt had collected a female "Medusa spider" whose bite could paralyze for eight hours and whose pheromones would attract every male spider on the island.

Back on the island, Hurley, Sawyer, Charlie, and Sun look over Nikki's body and try and decipher what she said. Charlie finds "gunk" under her fingernails and presumes she was digging and burying something. After much discussion, the words that Nikki muttered were determined to not be "power lines" or "plywood," as they once thought, but "Paulo lies." The group finds Paulo lying lifeless in the jungle with a shoe missing and his pants undone; Jin presumes the "Monster" did this to him.

The last flashback that occurs eight hours earlier shows Nikki finding the nicotine gum that she had believed to be lost in the same bag as the diamonds while Paulo is secretly retrieving the diamonds. Putting two and two together, Nikki confronts Paulo and throws the Medusa spider on him. After Paulo is bitten and paralysis sets in, Nikki looks for the diamonds by taking off his shoe first, and then finds the diamonds in Paulo's pants. She asks Paulo why he hid the truth from her, to which he responded, "If you found the diamonds, you wouldn't need me anymore." However, just as Dr. Arzt had predicted, a group of male Medusa spiders converge on Nikki and bite her in the leg. The first scene is then reenacted with Nikki running through the jungle, burying the diamonds, and collapsing by Sawyer and Hurley. However, this time her response to "What's wrong?" can be heard as "paralyzed..." not "Paulo lies." The last scene shows Nikki opening her eyes just as sand is thrown on her face during her and Paulo's burial. Paulo and Nikki are buried alive.

Like Paulo, sometimes we hide the truth from others. While this may seem like the right thing to do, whether it is to save someone from being hurt by the truth or to save yourself from getting in trouble, in the long run it won't help you or them. This can be seen in the Biblical story of

Sawyer: "Crime scene? There a forensics hatch I don't know about?"

Ananias and Sapphira.

In Acts 5:1-10, we can see the story of Ananias and Sapphira pan out. Ananias and Sapphira sold their possessions and, like the rest of the local Christians, were going to donate all of that to the disciples. However, they decided to keep a portion for themselves and hide the truth from Peter. Ananias gave Peter the donation, but Peter called him out and Ananias fell over dead. A few hours later, Peter confronts Sapphira about how much their possessions were worth. She openly lied and immediately fell over dead like her late husband. They both felt no guilt and decided to hide the truth from the disciples and God, and paid a steep price.

Like Ananias and Sapphira, we hide the truth sometimes. This, however, will, more often than not, lead to guilt. Guilt is that little needle poking you when you know you have done something wrong. Actually, guilt is the Holy Spirit letting you know what is right and what is wrong and what you have to atone for. Guilt is not a bad thing though. It is a sign that the Holy Spirit is in you and that He is convicting you to do right. It's up to you whether you bottle it up or let it go. The latter is the much better choice though since it brings relief or, as the adage goes, "the truth will set you free."

Sometimes you might think you are being a good friend if you hide something hurtful from someone. While our intentions are noble, so were Paulo's. Look where that got him. If the other person discovers what you've known and been hiding from them, they might not be so understanding (like Nikki). If we genuinely care about the other person, we should let them know, even if it might not be what they want to hear. Honesty is the sign of a true friend. Likewise,

Nikki: "Razzle Dazzle"

if we are hiding something from someone because we are afraid of how they would respond, we are implying that we don't have that much faith in that person to be understanding. If that person cares about you, they will be understanding. In the end, honesty is the best policy.

Is there anything that causes you guilt? Remember that all you have to do is confess to God, and He promises to forgive you, no matter what.

_____

_____

_____

Would you consider yourself an "open book"? Why or why not?

If you do hide a lot of things from people, why?

The Truth Comes Out

Prairie Lawyer

"There is a vague popular belief that lawyers are necessarily dishonest. ...Let no young man choosing the law for a calling for a moment yield to the popular belief—resolve to be honest at all events; and if in your own judgment you cannot be an honest lawyer, resolve to be honest without being a lawyer."

A. Lincoln
circa 1850

Picture by Denise Krebs

"If you have integrity, nothing else matters. If you don't have integrity, nothing else matters."
– Alan Simpson

Chapter 15

■ ■ ■

Not by Choice, but by Calling

Episode 15
"Left Behind"

"The Others" gas Kate, Jack, Sayid and Juliette, leaving them behind. They all wake up in different spots on the island. Kate and Juliette are handcuffed together when they wake up and are forced to work together to find the main camp. They look for Sayid and Jack. Once they found them back where "the Others" lived, all four of them travel together looking for the camp and their friends. Since all of them are missing from the camp, a leader is lacking among the group. Back at the camp though, Hurley cons Sawyer into being the leader of the group by telling him that the group was going to have a vote. This vote was about Sawyer. They were planning on voting Sawyer out of the camp and banishing him to another part of the island. This motivated Sawyer, making him want to change into the person and the leader that the group needed.

Being a leader is not easy. People will not always like you, the choices you make or the things you do. Sawyer was not respected very much by the people on the island, considering that they were going to maybe banish him from being with them. He had to "work his way up the ladder" and win them over. Sawyer even looks like a leader, someone who knows how to take control and lead a group of people. But he abused that power and it took Hurley to wake him up and to make him realize that he needed to change. He had to prove to the rest of the group that he was indeed capable of being a good leader and a nice person, and not always so sarcastic with everyone. He tried to make amends with everyone, apologizing to them and being nicer. A leader needs to know when it is a time to be serious, or a time to have fun. He needs to know how to make the right decisions for the better of the group. A leader should not leave anyone behind and should treat others well, and be trustworthy. A good leader has strong confidence and desires to be in the position they are in; they show dedication. Sawyer possesses some of these qualities, but not all. He did not want to be the leader of the group at first. Sawyer definitely has this same thing in common with Joshua in the Bible.

In Joshua 1, Moses, the great leader and faithful servant of God, dies. God then commands Joshua to take his place as leader and to lead the people into the land God had promised them. Then in Joshua 1:6-7, God says to Joshua, "Be strong and courageous, because you will lead these people to inherit the land I swore to their forefathers to give them. Be strong and very courageous." A few verses later God again says to Joshua, "Have I not commanded you? Be strong and courageous. Do not be terrified, do not be discouraged, for the Lord your God will be with you wherever you go." Even though it does not flat out say that Joshua did not want to be the leader, it kind of implies it that he was a bit fearful. To Joshua, God says, "Be strong and courageous" three times in one passage. He also tells Joshua to not be terrified and to not be discouraged because He would be with him wherever he went. Not only that, but in Deuteronomy 31, Moses addresses Joshua saying, "Be strong and courageous". He then says in verse 8, "The Lord himself goes before you and will be with you; he

Hurley: "But wasn't it nice being nice?"

will never leave you nor forsake you. Do not be afraid; do not be discouraged." God telling him these things implies that Joshua was fearful of being the leader and doing the things God had commanded him to do. Moses even said these same things to him before he died. God was letting Joshua know that he would take care of him as the leader.

Like Joshua, Sawyer seemed a bit reluctant. He did not necessarily want to be the leader. Just like Israel was in need of a new leader after Moses' death, the group on the island was in need of Sawyer as their leader. Sawyer knew that leadership was needed because Jack, Sayid, and Kate were gone. Just like any human, Sawyer is not perfect, but he was fit for that role. Joshua was fit for his role as well because God had placed him in that position for a reason. Although Sawyer was conned into being the leader, it ended up being rewarding in the end and he realized that that position was for him.

> Sawyer: "I just came by to say, your baby's... he's not as wrinkly as he was a couple weeks ago."

As followers of Christ, we can look at Joshua's life and learn from it. Many of us are fearful and lack confidence. But we can know that with God on our side, we are safe in his hands. We do not need to be afraid or discouraged, but instead, be strong and courageous. Confidence in Christ ultimately leads to having strength and courage in whatever you do. Leadership can be challenging, but God uses all of us in different ways to be leaders. We must do it in the right way, and that is exactly what Sawyer was trying to do. As Jim Rohn once said, "The challenge of leadership is to be strong, but not rude; be kind, but not weak; be bold, but not bully; be thoughtful, but not lazy; be humble, but not timid; be proud, but not arrogant; have humor, but without folly." Paul challenged Timothy, "For God did not give us a spirit of timidity, but a spirit of power, of love and of self-discipline" (2 Timothy 1:7). Power, love and self-discipline really encompass the effectiveness of a leader.

Do you feel like God has ever called you to leadership, but you were too scared to do it?

_____

_____

_____

_____

Why were you scared?

_____

_____

_____

_____

What are some ways God can use you in different areas of your life to lead?

_____

_____

_____

_____

Not by Choice, but by Calling

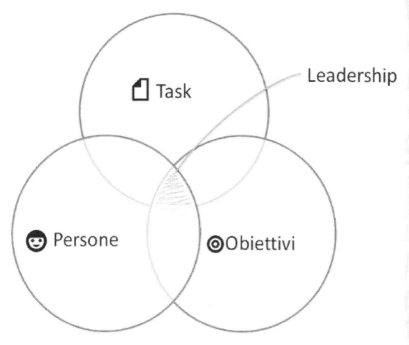

Picture by Luigi Mengato
(Obiettivi is Italian for Objectives)

"If your actions inspire others to dream more, learn more, do more and become more, you are a leader."
– John Quincy Adams

Chapter 16

■ ■ ■

Two-Faced

Episode 16
"One of Us"

Episode sixteen begins with Jack, Sayid, Kate, and Juliette tracking back to camp, after being gassed and left by "the Others." Sayid is on Juliet's case the whole way back, questioning who she is and what her people are doing on the island. Jack becomes angry with Sayid for this, and informs him that she will answer his questions when she is ready. In a flashback, Juliet is offered a job doing research with a company that she does not know anything about, called Mittelos Bioscience. Ethan and Richard tell her they are going to fly her away for her studies. In order to do this, they report that they must first tranquilize her, because the flight is a rough one. She begins to find the situation slightly sketchy, even though she already signed paperwork, agreed to avoid contact with people for six months, and has not even heard of their company. The tranquilizer causes Juliet to instantly pass out, and when she wakes up, they are already at their destination: the island.

Back to the present, Claire is starting to become very ill, which is worrying many people. Jack and the crew also return to camp at this point, which greatly relieves everyone. Claire soon passes out, and Juliet recalls that Ethan kidnapped and injected her back when she was pregnant, which might be causing her sudden illness. Juliet realizes that without more injection, Claire could very possibly die. Luckily, she knows where there is more injection fluid in a case, so she makes an offer to Jack to go get it, after explaining the whole situation. Everyone else is strongly against the idea, but Jack strongly trusts Juliet and tells her to go. In another flashback, Juliet begs Ben to let her leave the island, but he of course refuses. He says if she stays he will cure her sister's cancer, even though she finds that impossible since he himself has a cancerous tumor on his spine. He however does keep his promise,

> "Um, you probably shouldn't have drank that so fast."

and shows Juliet a video of her healed sister at the park with her child that Juliet helped produce. Sayid and Sawyer try to stop Juliet from getting the case, because they are still against the fact that she is one of "the Others." She confronts them with this, though, and tells them to stop trying to be leaders when neither of them can even pretend to be righteous, because of their past actions. In shock, she runs away with the case, and cures Claire with the injection. The episode ends with a conversation in the past between Juliet and Ben, and it clues us into the fact that Juliet is faking and is still one of "them," not one of Jack's.

Faking righteousness, or being a half-hearted Christian, is a problem that many believers have in today's society. They want to love God, but do not want to live life like Christ. Jonah struggled with this in the Bible, because he did not want to perform a task that God had in store for his life. God wanted him to do missions in Nineveh, a very sinful town. Instead, however, Jonah took a boat the opposite direction, because he did not trust in God's plan for his life, yet he pretended like he was a righteous man of the Lord. You cannot fake with God. He knows your heart, whether

> "Three men and a baby. I counted Hugo twice."
> Sawyer

other people do or not. As Christians, we are either all in or hardly in at all. In Revelation, John writes on being neither hot nor cold, but lukewarm. Revelation 3:16 states, "So, because you are lukewarm—neither hot nor cold—I am about to spit you out of my mouth." God gave up everything for us. He loves us, and the least we could do is be devout Christians. Following God comes with trials, of course, but the results are absolutely astounding. God can fill us up more than any new car or technological advancement. He is our biggest fan and our greatest encourager.

Isaiah 33:15 says "He who walks righteously and speaks uprightly, He who despises the gain of oppressions, Who gestures with his hands, refusing bribes, Who stops his ears from hearing of bloodshed, and shuts his eyes from seeing evil: He will dwell on high; his place of defense will be the fortress of rocks." This verse brings on another discipline: self examination. Moliere once said, "One should examine oneself for a very long time before thinking of condemning others." Watching our own steps, gestures and even thoughts should be our first concern. Then we can help others.

> Juliet: "If you can cure cancer, then why do you have it?"

Think back to the verse in Revelation. Do you feel like your relationship with God is genuine, or are you in a lukewarm relationship?

_____

_____

_____

_____

The famous saying "actions speak louder than words" is exhibited in this episode. Do you think others can see Jesus through your daily conversation and actions? Are you being a light for others to experience God?

_____

_____

_____

_____

What are some things, emotions, or people that may be keeping you from a full-fledged relationship with God? Reflect on these.

_____

_____

Challenge yourself to live out your Christian life and pursue your relationship with God with 100% effort, not in a lukewarm fashion.

Picture by Evalia England

"Your religion is what you do when the sermon is over."
– Quoted in P.S. I Love You

Chapter 17

■ ■ ■

Heads I Win, Tails You Lose

Episode 17
"Catch 22"

The episode starts off with Desmond, Hurley, Charlie and Jin walking through the jungle and having fun together in the rain. However, Charlie steps on one of Danielle's traps and is impaled through the throat with an arrow. Desmond can only watch as Charlie inevitably dies. Desmond comes to his senses, and it is revealed that what was just seen was another vision or flash of Charlie's death. Desmond also had flashes in which he saw Hurley finding a cable on the beach, a blinking light in the night sky, a parachutist hanging from a tree, a picture of Penny, and him and Penny reuniting. Desmond then goes about rounding up all of the other members of the group that he saw in the vision (Charlie, Hurley, and Jin) in order to ensure that the flash comes true by saying they are going on a camping trip along the beach.

Once on their trek, Hurley recognizes the spot where he first saw the cable and finds it again, just like in Desmond's vision. Desmond suggests they make camp for the night in order to see the next order of events, which occurs at night. Sure enough, after Jin scares Hurley with a Korean ghost story, a helicopter can be heard in the distance before crashing far out in the water. However, the same red light that Desmond previously saw is seen blinking in the night sky through the clouds. Charlie begins to grow suspicious of Desmond, who recently found the picture of Penny tucked into the parachutist's backpack. Desmond is now convinced that the parachutist has to be Penny just as it starts to rain. Hurley and Charlie then have the same conversation as the one at the start of the episode, but when Charlie steps on the trap, instead of sacrificing Charlie, Desmond tackles him in order to save him from the arrow. The group then finds the parachutist hanging from a tree, and Desmond believes that, by saving Charlie and his flash not coming true, he

> Sawyer: "What? My doorbell busted again?"

has killed Penny. However, upon taking off her helmet, the parachutist is an unknown woman who can only mutter, "Desmond," before passing out.

Flashbacks show Desmond becoming a monk after leaving his fiancé one week before their wedding. After a failed attempt to explain his decision to his ex-fiancé, Desmond is caught drinking the wine the monastery packages. Desmond is then released from his services, but is asked to help pack up the last of the wine. It is while packing the wine that he meets Penny for the first time, who gives him a ride home.

> Ruth: "We dated for six years and the closest you ever came to a religious experience was Celtics winning the cup."

The term "Catch-22" refers to a lose-lose situation where the outcome is always bad. In Desmond's case, his catch-22 was if he wants to be reunited with Penny, Charlie must die, or if he saves Charlie, he might not be reunited with Penny. Desmond points out to Brother Campbell that Moriah is a strange name for a monastery since that is where Abraham was to sacrifice Isaac. Brother Campbell responds that God ended up sparing Isaac, and it was a necessary test of faith and lesson in sacrifice.

In Genesis 22, God tells Abraham to go to

Moriah and sacrifice his only son, Isaac. Upon arriving in Moriah, Isaac asked why they had wood for the sacrifice, but no sacrifice. Abraham replied that God will provide the sacrifice. Abraham built the altar and tied Isaac down to it. As Abraham lifted his knife to sacrifice Isaac, God called out to him and said that since Abraham was willing to sacrifice his son, he now knows that Abraham loved and feared him. God then sent a ram for Abraham to sacrifice instead.

Early in the episode, Desmond chooses to not tell Charlie about his upcoming death in order to be with Penny and, consequently, makes Charlie his sacrifice. However, when push comes to shove, he could not sacrifice his friend, and paid the consequences. While we probably will not have to sacrifice our friend or be told by God to sacrifice our children, we are guaranteed to go through trials that test our faith. These trials are what build our faith in God by leaning on Him in times of need. As it says in Psalm 34:18-19, "The Lord is close to the brokenhearted and saves those who are crushed in spirit. The righteous person may have many troubles, but the Lord delivers him from them all." God puts difficulties in our lives to show that we need him, but he does not make us go through these trials alone. He is always by our side and watching over us.

Another person who had to go through a huge trial was Job. All but three of his servants were killed, all of his animals were killed, all of his children were killed, and he was afflicted with boils from head to toe. Even in all of this, he never cursed God for his misfortune and stayed loyal to him. He even praised God during it all. Job is a prime example of how to handle a trial that God presents before you. At all times in your life, through the good and the bad, God should be the one you lean on and the one you always praise. When we trust God, we never really are in a catch 22.

Hurley: "Dude, even if I spoke Korean it wouldn't make any sense."

Are there any trials you are going through right now? If so, have you been depending on God for strength?

_____

_____

_____

_____

Do you remember a time in the past when you realized God's help? Are you being a light for others to experience God?

_____

_____

_____

_____

Is God the first person you turn to when you need help in a situation?

_____

_____

_____

_____

Picture by Bernjan

"Faith is taking the first step even when you can't see the whole staircase."
— Martin Luther King, Jr

Chapter 18

■ ■ ■

D.O.H. (Date of Hope)

Episode 18
"D.O.C."

In the beginning of the episode, Jack was worried about Sun so he went to check up on her. He asked her a couple of questions about her health and how she was feeling. Sun was wondering why Jack was caring so much about her and how her health was, so she went and asked Kate about what happened to Jack when he was captured by "the Others." Kate told Sun that she should go talk to Juliet because she was a doctor for the pregnant people for "the Others." So Sun walks over to Juliet and asks what happens to pregnant people on this island. Juliet says if they get pregnant on the island they all die, but if they get pregnant off the island they will live. Kate takes Sun away before anything else happens. Later on, Juliet goes up to Sun and tells her about the secret place where she can determine if Sun got pregnant on or off the island. Sun's D.O.C. (date of conception) was important for another reason. If Sun got pregnant off the island it was because of an affair when she was cheating on Jin. It could only be Jin's child if she got pregnant on the island. While Sun and Juliet were walking to the secret hatch, Sun felt like telling Juliet why she was hoping she got pregnant on the Island even though she would die. They walk into the hatch, into a secret room with an ultrasound machine to tell when Sun got pregnant. The machine tells her that her D.O.C. was on the Island.

Jin's mother: "Really? Did you know he was also the son of a prostitute?"

Sun's flashback is when she talks to Jin about how much she loves him and he loves her. When she is finished talking to him, she hangs up and sits down next to a stranger. The person asks if a picture in the newspaper was her. Sun says yes and that she just got married to a lovely man. The stranger asks if her family is really powerful. Sun agrees, but wonders why she asked. The stranger blackmails her, informing her she is going to marry the son of a fisherman, which would bring shame on the family. The cost of silence would be $100,000. The stranger tells her to meet back in three days. When Sun gets home, she asks about Jin's family. He says their all dead. Sun is not satisfied and goes out to find Jin's father. She asks Jin's father about Jin's secrecy about his father, mother and past. Jin's father tells Sun that Jin's mother was a prostitute and is the stranger who is threatening her and demanding money. Sun leaves and goes to her father for money to keep what her husband family a secret from everyone. Sun's father tells her to leave him or leave the country. Sun grabs the money, pays Jin's mother and asks what type of mother would do this to their son. Jin mother says that she is not his mother even though she gave birth to him.

In the Bible, we see multiple examples of hope in seemingly hopeless situations. Rahab was a prostitute, but she helped the Israelites, thus, she was spared from the bloodshed at Jericho. Boaz was a man who helped a woman named Ruth. Ruth had no future after her husband and father-in-law both died. King David was a man who went against insurmountable odds in many occasions. First he killed

Sun: "I love you madly."

a bear and a lion to protect his sheep. He killed a giant, Goliath, with a small stone and a sling. When David sinned against God he repented and came back to the Lord. All of these people are great examples of hope. All these people are in the genealogy

Jin's Mother "I gave birth to him, but that does not make me his mother."

of Jesus Christ, our Savior (Matthew 1:1-17). If God can make a future out of all these sinful and hopeless people, then why not give God a chance. Hope is a gift that one receives from God to persist in trials and not surrender. Ask Him to give you hope. If He chose these people as the ancestors of Jesus how much more will He do for you?

Hope is also about something in the next life. Hope is worthless if there is not an end goal or motivation. As Christians, our hope is in eternal life. Because, of Christ we can have this hope and be certain of eternal life. 1 Corinthians 15:19-20 says, "If only for this life we have hope in Christ, we are of all people most to be pitied. But Christ has indeed been raised from the dead, the firstfruits of those who have fallen asleep." A hope goes beyond this life - it is forever. Psalm 9:18 is powerful in meaning, showing that God cares for the greatest and least: "But the needy will not always be forgotten, nor the hope of the afflicted ever perish." Finally, a verse that should be memorized by all believers of Jesus Christ: "'For I know the plans I have for you,' declares the LORD, 'plans to prosper you and not to harm you, plans to give you hope and a future.'" God has a plan for you. It involves words like prosper and hope. We are blessed.

Are there things in life that you doubt? What are they?

___

___

___

___

What things are taking away your hope in life?

___

___

___

___

What is your definition of hope?

What gives you hope?

D.O.H. (Date of Hope)

Picture by Pol Sifter

"We must accept finite disappointment, but never lose infinite hope."
– Martin Luther King, Jr

Chapter 19
■ ■ ■

Brigantino

Episode 19
"The Brig"

Locke tries to get Sayid to come with him and kill Ben (who Locke captured). Then he asks Sawyer to come along, who originally refuses but eventually comes along. Locke knows everything that is in Sawyer's file and what happened in his past. Locke says he cannot kill Ben and that is why he wants Sawyer to do it. Sawyer and Locke reach a large slave ship called the Black Rock. Sawyer says he will not kill anyone so Locke locks him in a room with "Ben" who is tied up with a bag over his head. When Sawyer pulls the bag off, he sees that it is Locke's father. Sawyer and Locke's father discuss why Locke has him tied up. During their conversation, Locke's father lists all of

Anthony: "A little hot for Heaven, isn't it?"

his con names. He mentions Tom Sawyer, and Sawyer realizes that this might be the man who caused his parents' deaths. Sawyer then makes Locke's father read the note he has had sense he was a little boy. Locke's dad makes a joke about the con and Sawyer parents' death. Locke's dad rips up the letter, and Sawyer chokes him to death with a chain. Later, Locke tells Sawyer that Juliet is a fake and gives him the tape she recorded in the medical center. Sawyer then returns to the camp and Locke returns to "the Others" with his father's dead body. Meanwhile on the island, loyalties are tested because no one trusts Juliet, and now even Jack, because he is hanging around Juliet. Locke and Sawyer had a hard time accepting their past, while the survivors have a hard time accepting Juliet and Jack.

A Bible character who experiences difficulty with being accepted is the Samaritan woman who meets Jesus at the well in Samaria. The Samaritan woman comes to the well at noon, rather than the usual time when other woman would go to draw water. The reason for why she comes at a different time is later given in the chapter. Jesus told her, "Go, call your husband and come back." Her response sounds innocent as she says she has no husband. But, Jesus knew her story. He said to her, "You are right when you say you have no husband. The fact, you have had five husbands, and the man you now have is not your husband. What you have just said is quite true" (John 11:16-18). The woman had been with many men and had gained some kind of reputation that has caused her to become a social pariah. The woman avoids the other women at the well, perhaps, to avoid disapproving stares and whispers. The woman is not accepted by her fellow Samaritans, but Jesus begins to speak to the woman. She is shocked, and the first thing she says to him is, "You are a Jew and I am a Samaritan woman, how can you ask me for a drink" (John 4:9)? The verse even subtitles that Jews did not associate with Samaritans. Because Jesus was a Jew, it was surprising for him to acknowledge a Samaritan. In addition, Jesus knew about this woman and what she has done. However, that did not stop Jesus from offering the woman eternal life, "Everyone who drinks this water will be thirsty again, but whoever drinks the water I give him will never thirst. Indeed the water I give

> "You're wasting your time, bug eye," Anthony says, "me and him have been through all this. All he wants is his daddy."

him will become in him a spring of water welling up to eternal like" (John 11:13-14). Jesus still accepts the woman for who she is - a Samaritan and an adulterous- even when her own people would not. Eventually, the disciples, as well, are accepting of this woman. It says in John 4:27, "Just then his disciples returned and were surprised to find him talking with a woman. But no one asked," What do you want?' or "Why are you talking to her?" Even disciples accepted the Samaritan woman. As a result, the woman believed Jesus when he told her who he was, the Messiah. After the disciples returned to Jesus, the woman left her water jar (the reason she was at the well) to tell the people in the town about Jesus. Surprisingly, the people in the town believed the woman and went to see Jesus.

Acceptance is known to be a foundational need for everyone. Romans 15:7 says, "Accept one another, then, just as Christ accepted you, in order to bring praise to God." Jesus was willing to talk to a Samaritan, even a Samaritan woman, and even an adulterous. He accepted her. Likewise, he accepts us. Just as we have received His acceptance, we should accept each other. The result is praise to God.

Naomi: "Remind me not to rescue you, Sayid"

John 13:20 refers to Jesus sending out people, "I tell you the truth, whoever accepts anyone I send accepts me; and whoever accepts me accepts the one who sent me." We need to view people in our lives as being sent by God. He has a plan and a reason. In accepting them, we accept Him.

Who do you have a hard time with?

_____

_____

_____

_____

Why is it such a struggle?

_____

_____

_____

_____

What should you do to start being more accepting of them?

_____

_____

_____

_____

What gives you hope?

_____

_____

_____

_____

Brigantino | 151

Picture by Norma Thomas

"The curious paradox is that when I accept myself just as I am, then I can change."
– Carl Rogers

Chapter 20

■ ■ ■

"The Blame Game"

Episode 20
"The Man Behind the Curtain"

In this episode of Lost, we begin to learn about the history of Ben. Baby Ben was born in the woods of Portland, Oregon. His mother (Emily Linus) died due to complications with childbirth. This explains why Ben's father (Roger Linus) blames him for the death of his wife. This episode also reveals that Ben was not born on the island, but moved there in 1973 with his father. During his childhood on the island, Ben experiences one of the "skirmishes" with "The Others" and the members of the DHARMA Initiative have. Roger's neglect caused Ben to turn away for the DHARMA

> Locke: "You are the man behind the curtain, the Wizard of Oz. And you're a liar."

Initiative and side with "The Others." Eventually, Ben kills his father, while "The Others" kill the rest of the DHARMA Initiative.

"We all answer to someone" Ben

Back on the island, Sawyer and Sayid discuss the recently discovered tape recording of Juliet. They intend to blame Juliet for the upcoming trouble facing the camp. Ben and the rest of "The Others'" camp are astounded at the return of Locke with the corpse of his father. Ben begins to explain to Locke that it is not he who is in control but someone named Jacob. Locke then calls Ben a liar and manipulates Ben into taking him to Jacob. When they reach their destination, a rundown cabin, Locke sees there is no one inside, yet Ben appears to be talking to someone. Locke gets annoyed by the apparent charade, and upsets Jacob which causes Locke and Ben to flee the cabin. The next morning, Ben asks if Locke heard anything. Locke responds by calling Ben a liar. As they continue their trek, Ben explains to Locke that he has not been completely truthful, and, in the past, had to choose a side. At this point, Ben revels to Locke the mass grave of the former DHARMA Initiative members. Then Ben shoots Locke leaving him for dead but not before asking what Jacob said. To which Locke responds, "Help me."

Through the majority of the episode, blame is a main theme. When Ben was born, his mother died in child birth. Later on, once Ben has grown up, his father continues to blame Ben for the death of his wife. This blame lingers throughout Ben's entire life, until Ben kills his father. Blame can lead to anger and anger can lead to uncontrollable emotion which can ruin one's life .This is exemplified with Ben and his relationship with his father.

Blaming comes naturally and easily for us humans. As a matter of fact, blame began at the beginning of time! When God asked Adam about his sin, he pointed his finger at Eve (Genesis 3:12): "The man said, 'The woman you put here with me—she gave me some fruit from the tree, and I ate it.'" When God came to Eve and confronted her about her sin, she blamed the serpent (Genesis 3:13): "Then the LORD God said to the woman, 'What is this you have done?' The woman said, 'The serpent deceived me, and I ate.'" Although there is a line of blame going on in this story of The Fall of Man, all were still punished by God in the end (Genesis 3:14-23). When we attempt to shift our issues upon someone else with blame, we are still guilty and held accountable. 2 Corinthians 5:10 tells us that we will all answer before God and receive what is due to us in the end no matter what: " For we must all appear before the judgment seat of Christ, that each one may receive what is due him for the things done while in the body, whether good or bad."

"Well I guess there's a first time for everything"- Locke

Further down the line in the New Testament, Jesus tells the disciples at The Lord's Supper that one of them will betray him. Immediately following the sad news, the disciples react with a panicked, "Surely not I, Lord?" (Matthew 26: 21-22). The disciples had an attitude towards Jesus' bad news of the betrayal by claiming it to be not their problem, but someone else's. This is how blame goes. When we have a problem, blaming is not the choice to resort to (neither is murder). Galatians 6:5 tells us that each one should carry his own load. The whole verse is a simple little line, "For each one should carry his own load." How could one do this if he continually shoved his own load upon others?

How do you deal with blame?

_____

_____

_____

_____

Do you blame problems on others?

_____

_____

_____

_____

Do you do a good job of carrying your own load?

_____

_____

_____

_____

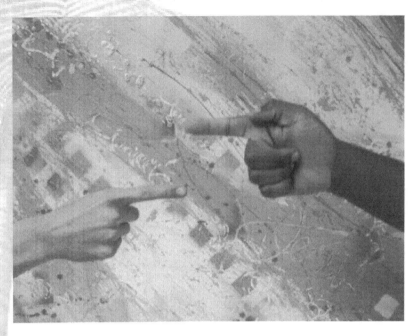

Picture by Adam Exelby and Ryan Evans

"A man can get discouraged many times but he is not a failure until he begins to blame somebody else and stops trying."
– John Burroughs

Chapter 21

■ ■ ■

Count Your Many Blessings

Episode 21
"Greatest Hits"

Desmond has another one of his flashes. This time he sees Charlie drowning. Charlie has to come to grips with the fact that he is going to die. Knowing that he is going to die, he creates a "Greatest List" sheet where he writes down his top five blessings in his life. As he is writing down his top five, he has flashbacks about them and recaps them in his mind. He starts off with number five being the time when he first heard himself on the radio. The flashback starts off when he and his fellow band members are driving on the road when their car breaks down. They get out of the car to check out the damage when all of a sudden their song starts to play on the radio. They all are full of joy and begin to go celebrate. Number four was when his dad taught him to swim for the first time. It shows Charlie at a young age standing on the edge of the pool while his dad is telling him to jump in. His dad is insisting that he will catch him, so Charlie jumps in and his dad taught him how to swim that day. Next he writes down number three which is when Charlie's brother Liam gives him the family ring that has their great-grandfathers initials on it. At first Charlie does not take it, but eventually he does. Number 2 on the list is when Charlie saves the woman in the alley from being mugged. Charlie was on his way home when he heard the woman screaming and being mugged. Charlie rushed in and made the thief run away. The woman called him a hero and that was the end of the flashback. Charlie's number one on the list was when he met Claire on the island. It was shortly after the plane crash and Charlie noticed her sitting by herself by the broken plane. He goes over with a blanket in his hand and offers it to her. She accepts and the two begin to talk.

> Charlie: "I'll do it. I'll swim down, flip that bloody switch, swim back up. Piece of cake."

Charlie, knowing that he was going to die, made a list of all the major blessings in his life. He could reminisce in these memories and be thankful for what he had experienced all throughout the years before it was too late. And that is exactly what he did. However, in Exodus 16, we find the Israelites complaining. They complain against Moses and Aaron because their food supplies were running out while on their journey. In verse 12 it says, "The LORD said to Moses, 'I have heard the grumbling of the Israelites. Tell them, 'At twilight you will eat meat, and in the morning you will be filled with bread. Then you will know that I am the LORD your God.'" But, yet, what did God do? He gave them manna. He blessed them, even through their complaining. The Israelites were in a bad situation: they were running out of food. Charlie was in a bad situation as well: he would be facing death very shortly. But how did Charlie and the Israelites react differently? Charlie could have complained and carried on and on about how it was not fair that it was his time to die. But instead, he did something different. Charlie knew that death would be coming eventually, so that is why he took the time to go over his many blessings throughout his life and be thankful. Instead of complaining, he only wrote the blessings that he had received.

The Israelites had much for which to be thankful. They were free, no longer slaves of Egypt. They were given gold and valuables from the Egyptians. God was leading them. They crossed the Red Sea, even on dry ground. Their enemies were killed in the Red Sea. God fed them daily with Manna. Their clothes and scandals didn't wear out. They were blessed, but complained.

Since Charlie knew death was coming soon, he wrote down his top five "greatest hits" or "greatest blessings." But, as Christians, should we only be thanking God for all our blessings right before we are about to die? God blesses us each and every day, and we should acknowledge the fact more often. In John 1:16 it says, "From the fullness of his grace we have all received one blessing after another." This is so very true! Sometimes it may not feel like blessings are being "showered over you," but if you think hard enough, God has blessed you in many ways, in ways you might not have even noticed. It can be difficult to be thankful in trying situations, like Charlie's situation. He knew that he would be heading for death soon enough, yet he wrote down his blessings and was calm in doing so. The song "Count your blessings" sums it all up. The song goes:

> Naomi: "No, not that. The crash. You're the dead rock star. They made a big deal out of you when they found plane. Huge memorial service, new album--"

Count Your Many Blessings

"When upon life's billows you are tempest tossed,
When you are discouraged thinking all is lost,
Count your many blessings, name them one by one,
And it will surprise you what the Lord hath done.
Are you ever burdened with a load of care?
Does the cross seem heavy you are called to bear?
Count your many blessings, every doubt will fly,
And you will be singing as the days go by.
So, amid the conflicts, whether great or small,
Do not be discouraged, God is over all;
Count your many blessings, angels will attend,
Help and comfort give you to your journey's end.
Count your blessings, name them one by one;
Count your blessings, see what God hath done;
Count your blessings, name them one by one;
Count your many blessings, see what God hath done."

Try counting your blessings one by one. It helps you focus on the good things, and put the bad things in the right perspective.

What are some things you complain about?

How is it better to have a positive outlook on things rather than to complain about them?

List some ways in which God has blessed you in your life and even TODAY.

Count Your Many Blessings

Picture by Rebecca Wilson

"Count your blessings instead of your crosses; Count your gains instead of your losses. Count your joys instead of your woes; Count your friends instead of your foes. Count your smiles instead of your tears; Count your courage instead of your fears. Count your full years instead of your lean; Count your kind deeds instead of your mean. Count your health instead of your wealth; Count on God instead of yourself."

– Author Unknown

Chapter 22

■ ■ ■

To Live To Die

Episode 22-23
"Through the Looking Glass"

Charlie becomes good friends with Desmond over the course of Lost season 3. The reason for their sudden friendship is Desmond's ability to see how Charlie is going to die, and he almost dies several times except for the help of Desmond. In one of the last episodes of the season, Desmond has a vision of Charlie drowning right before Claire, his girlfriend, gets on a helicopter leaving the island. Desmond convinces Charlie that the only way Claire will be able to get on the helicopter is if he follows the vision step by step. Charlie, in a wave of nostalgia, begins to write out his "greatest hits," the top of which is meeting Claire. When the time comes to swim down to the looking glass, the underwater base that is jamming all transmission signals coming in and leaving the island, Charlie tells Desmond that he is to deliver the list of key moments in his life to Claire when he returns to the island. Desmond offers to take Charlie's place so he can get off the island with Claire, but Charlie declines the proposal and knocks Desmond out so he will not swim down with him. When Charlie gets down to the Looking Glass, he finds two women protecting it. The two women proceed to tie Charlie to a chair and interrogate him about where he came from and how he found the Looking Glass. When Ben finds out that Charlie has made it to the Looking Glass he sends Mikhail to take care of things. Desmond comes to on the surface of the ocean and decides to swim after Charlie to see if he is doing alright in the Looking Glass. Desmond ends up hiding in a locker in the corner of the Looking Glasses interior. When Mikhail makes it to the Looking Glass, he kills one of the women who are interrogating Charlie and mortally wounds the other, after which Desmond steps out of the locker and shoots Mikhail with a harpoon gun. With her dying word, the wounded woman tells Charlie the code to shut off the Looking Glass' jammer.

> Charlie: "I came in my invisible submarine. Don't you see it?"

When Charlie puts in the code, Penelope, Desmond's ex-lover, comes on in a transmission. Just then, Mikhail shows up with a grenade and blows the window of the room Charlie is in, and in a desperate attempt to save the life of Desmond, seals himself in the room. With his dying breath Charlie tells Desmond that the boat that is waiting just offshore is, contrary to popular belief, not Penelope's.

Much like Charlie's sacrifice for the salvation of the other people on the island, Christ died for every single person who ever comes into existence in the hope that they may accept the reality of the ultimate Deity which is Christ, admit their sins and therefore their need for Christ's salvation, and submit to Him. There are countless accounts of Christ's famous sacrifice on the cross for the sins of man; however, very rarely is it ever noted that Christ gave His life, not in death, but while He was alive, for the sins of man. Christ made the ultimate sacrifice not in death, but in living a perfect life of love as an example for those who would follow Him.

Every single day Jesus bore a cross, not literally, but every day He went through hardships, temptations, and trials. The things that Jesus went through during his life would be far more than anyone could ever handle without committing a sin, without losing faith, without giving up. However, even though Jesus was constantly bombarded by demonic powers in an effort to make his existence meaningless and all of mankind hopeless of ever achieving the kind of salvation we can experience through God's grace today, Jesus still was able to grow stronger in His faith.

As Christ's life progressed, He began performing more and more impressive miracles and began to sacrifice more of his time for His Father's work. Towards the very end of Christ's life, during the last three years, He began to take on full-time ministry. However, before He became a full time missionary, He still embodied a lifestyle that was constantly honorable to God. He ministered through His actions of love. No matter where Jesus went, He was always striving to be gentle to everyone around Him, even those who had plans to murder Him. Jesus strived so much to be loving that He even asked God to pardon those who mocked Him while He was on the cross dying for their sins. Just as Charlie sacrificed himself for the salvation of the other people on the island, and just as Christ sacrificed his whole life for

> Rose: "If you say 'Live together, die alone,' to me, Jack, I'm going to punch you in the face."

the salvation of the world, Christians are called to a life of sacrifice. Even His sacrifice of stepping down from heaven to come to earth for us was astronomical. He came to earth for us to live for us, to die for us, so that He Himself would be the ultimate sacrifice in life and death for our sins. Every person who has ever sinned is therefore responsible for the death of Christ, and yet He still forgives and still loves us.

> Hurley: "Yeah, dude, we'll stay put until you, like, phone home."

We are called to live a life of faithful sacrifice to our Savior. We are commissioned to love no matter what the cost, to forgive no matter what the offense, and to go into every part of the world to share the news of the only true hope and salvation any person can ever have. Matthew 28:19-20 gives our directions, "Therefore go and make disciples of all nations, baptizing them in the name of the Father and of the Son and of the Holy Spirit, and teaching them to obey everything I have commanded you. And surely I am with you always, to the very end of the age." Even though Jesus sends out His followers into the world, He does not leave them alone. He promises to always be with us.

Have you placed your trust in Jesus Christ? If not why?

_____

_____

_____

_____

Are you striving to daily be a follower of Jesus?

_____

_____

_____

_____

Is there someone you know that hasn't placed their trust in Jesus? If so, who? Pray for them now. What should you do or say that could open up conversation about Jesus?

_____

_____

_____

_____

Picture by Kelsey

"The funny thing about worship is it only works if you actually do it."-
– Anonymous

About the Authors

Dr. Randy T. Johnson has been married to Angela for over 25 years. They have two children, Clint and Stephanie. He has been Chaplain and Bible teacher at Oakland Christian School in Auburn Hills, Michigan for 20 years. He also ministers at two local Chinese Church youth groups. He wrote And Then Some, created Read316.com., and co-authored LOST Lessons.

David Rutledge has been working in youth ministry for over 10 years as a Bible teacher, a youth pastor and a speaker. David has a degree in Biblical Studies/Christian Education of Youth and History from Cedarville University, a Masters of Education from Regent University and is currently finishing up his Doctorate of Education from Liberty University. David lives with his wife Rebekah and children in Burbank California. He co-authored LOST Lessons.

To order additional copies of **LOST** Lessons 3 or
to find out more by Dr. Randy Johnson,
David Rutledge or other life changing books
published by Rochester Media,
please visit our website **www.rochestermedia.com**

Discounts are available for ministry and
retail purposes.

Contact Rochester Media

Rochester Media LLC
P.O. Box 80002
Rochester, MI 48308
248-429-READ
info@rochestermedia.com

Made in the USA
Charleston, SC
14 November 2012